STANDING WITH PETER

STANDING WITH PETER

*Reflections of a Lay Moral Theologian
on God's Loving Providence*

BY

WILLIAM E. MAY

REQUIEM PRESS
BETHUNE, SC
2006

Cover Photo: from L'Osservatore Romano, used with permission.

REQUIEM PRESS
P.O. Box 7
Bethune, SC 29009
1-888-708-7675
www.RequiemPress.com

ISBN-10: 0-9788687-0-6
ISBN-13: 978-0-9788687-0-3

Library of Congress Control Number: 2006931683

Printed in the United States of America

By his providence God protects and governs everything he has made, "*reaching mightily from one end of the earth to the other, and ordering all things well*" (Wis 8.1).

To my wife, Patricia,
and
to my parents,
Robert W. May (died December 1, 1975)
and
Katherine A. May (died July 20, 1985)

CONTENTS

INTRODUCTION

When I was 40 years old in 1968 I never thought that during the 1970s and later I would play a role in defending the teaching of the Catholic Church on contraception and the existence of absolute moral norms protecting the inviolability of innocent human life, the goods of human sexuality, and of marriage. In fact, in 1968, God, through the mysterious workings of his providence, allowed me, principally because of pride and human respect, to sign the document dissenting from Pope Paul VI's encyclical *Humanae vitae*, in which he reaffirmed the Church's age-old teaching that contraception is an intrinsically disordered act. Signing this document was on my part a cowardly deed, but paradoxically and providentially doing so helped me get a job as a teacher of moral theology several years later.

I hope to show in this memoir how good God has been to me and how he has exercised his loving providence on my behalf. I believe that God, in his providence, prepared me remotely and proximately to present, explain, and defend the liberating truth of the Church's moral teaching—and then gave me the opportunity to do so. It is my hope is that this story will not only serve to thank God publicly for his great goodness to me but also encourage others to ask his pardon for whatever they have done or failed to do that offended him by the harm it caused and to remember that this loving Father, who sent his Son to redeem us, will not give his children a stone if they ask for bread but will rather give them the Bread of Life.

Chapter One

Early Years

I was born in St. Louis, Missouri, the second child of Robert W. May and Katherine A. Armstrong, on May 27, 1928. I was immediately baptized because I was a "premie," and there was serious danger that I would die. My older sister, Rosemary, had been born in 1926, and my younger sister, Virginia (Jincey), was born in 1932. Both of my sisters were—and are—very good to me, and I will say more of them later. My mother was a Catholic whose parents, William and Mary Armstrong, had emigrated as teenagers from Ireland to the United States. Before marrying Bill Armstrong, a St. Louis policeman, Mary, neé Hussey, had worked as a servant girl. She never did learn to read or write, but she knew how to pray, particularly the rosary, which she said in Gaelic every day. Her husband Bill died about the time I was born, and for the rest of her life my Irish grandmother lived with us. I was the apple of her eye. Her little "Billy" could do no wrong.

My father was not then a Catholic, but a Presbyterian; he truly carried out the father's task of "reliving and revealing on earth the very Fatherhood of God" (see Pope John Paul II, *Familiaris consortio*, 28). On occasions his mother, Rose Bailey May, whose husband William died before I was born, also lived with us. She was a great storyteller and loved to read books to my sisters and me and entertain us with some pretty tall tales. My father, who worked for the Standard Oil Company of Indiana, had been in World War I, and among the friends he had made in the army was a Catholic priest, Mark Carroll. Father Carroll was, at the time of my birth, pastor of St. Margaret of Scotland parish in south St. Louis. He was later rector of the "Old Cathedral" on the waterfront of St. Louis, and later still the first Bishop of Wichita. He also served as rector of the Cathedral Latin School, where young boys desiring to become priests studied during freshman and sophomore high school. Fr. Carroll also had a fantastic sense of Irish humor. I remember one evening when I was a little boy, probably about 8 years old, when he was at our home for dinner and he asked my parents if they knew who were the "five most constipated men" in the Bible. The answer: "Cain, because he wasn't Abel, Balaam, because he had trouble with his ass, Moses, because he took two tablets in the desert, David, because he sat on the throne for forty years, and Titus from the New Testament, because the name stands for itself." As you can see, these words of Biblical interpretation had a powerful effect on me, as I remember the story vividly close to seventy years later.

Another frequent visitor to our home at that time was Father Lloyd Sullivan, one of the priests at St. Margaret's. He was a strikingly handsome priest, obviously well educated, happy to be a priest and a welcome guest at dinner. I know that my father loved to engage him in conversation, particularly about Catholic teachings, and deeply appreciated his kindness, his love of Christ, and his friendship. Father Sullivan, I recall, told us that he thought Arnold Lunn's book, *Now I See*, was one of the best "conversion" books he knew of. Later in life I read this very excellent book, and I still think it a powerful and beautiful apologetic.

Our father took seriously his promise to raise his children in the Catholic faith. Each evening he would listen to my sisters and me recite our Baltimore Catechism lesson, so that I am sure that by the time we finished Catholic grammar school he knew what the Catholic Church taught as well as any baptized Catholic, if not better than most. Our mother was exceptionally pious and prayed every day for her husband's conversion and for her children's Catholic faith.

When I was born and for the early years of my childhood we lived in a four family flat in south St. Louis, although we moved from the flat to a nicer one-family home in the same parish about the time I was in kindergarten or first grade. Another family in the flat was that of my mother's sister, Mary, who had married a fine man of German descent, Joseph Witte. Aunt Mary was extremely "witty" and a lot of fun to be with; her personality then was a little like "I love Lucy's." Later in life she suffered from psychological problems (in all likelihood she was manic-depressive or bipolar). To cope with these problems, she eventually had a frontal lobotomy, which changed her from an outgoing individual to being somewhat lethargic and withdrawn. Aunt Mary and Uncle Joe had two children, Joseph Jr. whom we called Sonny, about 2 years younger than I, and Dolores, who was a bit younger than my sister Jincey. This was during the depths of the Great Depression; fortunately, my father had a good position with the Standard Oil Company of Indiana, but Uncle Joe had a hard time finding work. He took on all kinds of odd jobs to support his family; he was a man of deep Catholic faith. Eventually, my father was helpful in getting him a job with the Shell Oil Company in St. Louis, and my uncle remained with them until his retirement many years later. This was also during Prohibition years, and I can remember as a child stomping juice out of grapes in the basement for homemade wine.

When I was in second grade my father was made manager of the Standard Oil Company office in Decatur, Illinois. So we moved there and lived on the outskirts of the city; the land across the street at the time was a farm with plenty of sheep. We went to St. James Catholic Church and School for the two years we lived in Decatur. Decatur was at that time known as the "Soy Bean Capital of the World," or was it "of the United States," or perhaps only "of the State of Illinois." At any rate, soy beans were mighty high in Decatur at that time.

We returned to St. Louis when I was in fourth grade, about 1938, because my father had been made manager of the St. Louis division of the Standard Oil Company. We moved into a rented house in Richmond Heights, Missouri, a St. Louis suburb in the parish of St. Luke the Evangelist. The pastor of St. Luke's, Father Joseph McMahon, affectionately known as "Father Mac," was one of the holiest, kindest, and most wonderful priests I have ever known. He was not a very good preacher, but he loved his people and they loved him; in particular, he loved children. He was a great little athlete, playing soccer very well and excelling on ice skates. Fr. Mac loved to take as many schoolchildren as he could skating with him. Because he was such a holy priest, many of the boys from St. Luke's entered the seminary, and a large number of them went on to ordination, among them were Jack Kennedy, Fenton Runge, and the three Forst boys—Marion (who became bishop of Dodge City, Kansas), Charles, and my classmate, Bill. The assistant priests at St. Luke's were also wonderful men who loved the Church, the priesthood, and their parishioners. I remember in particular Father Joseph O'Toole and, later on, Father Robert Peet, fine men of God. The Sisters of St. Joseph of Carondelet taught in St. Luke's school, and my memories of them are wonderful. They were good teachers; many of them were exceptionally witty (Sister St. Peter in particular) and strict discipliners. The actress who stars in the contemporary humorous yet reverent play "Saturday Night Catechism" reminds me of these wonderful women, who radiated happiness. Some of them were also, in my mind, quite beautiful, even if one could only see their faces. I think that for a spell I actually had a boyish crush on my sixth-grade teacher, Sister David Marie.

Because these Sisters were so loving and good, I find most irritating the slanderous stories circulated about Catholic schools in the pre-Vatican II days and the Sisters who taught in them. The Sisters who taught us radiated happiness and love, so much so that my younger sister decided to become one of them after she graduated from high school and my father, at that time not even a Catholic, had the highest regard and respect for them.

From the time I was in fourth grade and for many, many years thereafter I wanted to become a priest. Originally, I longed to become a Maryknoll missioner to China, and I made regular visits to the Maryknoll house in St. Louis, at that time directed by a remarkable priest, Father Thomas Martin. So anxious was I to become a Maryknoll missioner in China that I even purchased a Chinese language textbook, but I did not make much headway with it. Yet I dreamed of serving Christ in China and pictured myself dying a martyr's death there.

About the time I graduated from St. Luke's we moved to our own home in Clayton, MO, near Richmond Heights. It was in the parish of Our Lady of Lourdes, but we continued going to St.

Luke's until many years later, after a new pastor, Msgr. Edward Rogers—another World War I veteran as a chaplain—became pastor. After graduation from St. Luke's I wanted to go to the seminary, but my parents wanted me to wait a bit and so sent me to Christian Brothers College (Christian Brothers Military High School) which was not too far from our new home and to which I could easily walk. Popularly known by its initials "CBC," it was called "Cry Babies' College" by many of my friends who went to St. Louis University High School. CBC was, however, a fine school, with an excellent academic program. My homeroom teacher, Brother Linus Albert, taught religion and Latin, and he did a great job. He was a big, powerful man who did not tolerate nonsense and who could talk turkey to adolescent males and show them tough love. When he learned that I wanted to be a priest he urged me to leave CBC after my freshman year and go to the Cathedral Latin School, at that time the "seminary" high school for the freshman and sophomore boys who aspired to the diocesan priesthood. At CBC all freshmen were required to take typing in addition to Latin, English, Algebra, etc. and I am most grateful that I learned this most useful skill then. I wish my own children had been forced to learn it in high school, because I later discovered that they wanted me to type their high school reports for them (in a way this too was a providential intervention, because in typing their papers I got to know a good deal of how they were thinking on some important issues). Eventually, they typed their own papers, thank goodness.

SEMINARY LIFE

My parents agreed to let me go to the "Latin" school for my second year of high school. At that time, as noted already, Msgr. Carroll was its rector, and we had some brilliant and talented priests of the archdiocese of St. Louis as our teachers. Among the most memorable in my book were Fathers Charles Helmsing, Carl Poelker, Fred Sprinke, Glennon Flavin, Jasper Chiodini, and Msgr. Mark Ebner. Father Helmsing taught us English and European history; he was a holy priest and an excellent teacher, who later in life became Archbishop of Kansas City, Missouri. We called him "cue-ball Charlie" because he was quite bald even as a young man, but we all respected him as a good role model for priests. Moreover, we learned a lot from him because he knew European history quite well and did a fine job of helping us write English decently. He also gave us a great love for the role the Church played in western civilization. Father Poelker taught religion and was the disciplinarian of the place, and he could be tough. Father Sprinke—he may have been a monsignor—taught Latin (in sophomore year we read Caesar's *Gallic Wars*) while pacing the room in a cassock marked with chalk. He had studied for the priesthood in Rome and could actually *speak* Latin! Glennon Flavin, who later became pastor of Our Lady of Lourdes Church in Clayton, MO where our family then lived and still later Bishop of Lincoln NE, also taught religion. I did not have him as a teacher, but I remember him as a young, very holy and zealous priest. Father Chiodini gave us a class in Italian once a week, and years later such useful phrases such as *"Dov'è il gabinetto"* ("Where's the bathroom?") and *"Chi ha un fiamifero?"* ("Who has a match?") were still in my memory. Msgr. Mark Ebner was a brilliant teacher of mathematics with the ability to arch his eyebrows when quizzing someone, but his eyes usually had a merry twinkle to them. All these priests were happy that they were priests and gave us good example.

My classmates at the Latin school and later at St. Louis Preparatory Seminary (now Glennon Preparatory Seminary) were a wonderful group of intelligent, fun-loving, morally good young fellows: Bill Forst (my classmate from St. Luke's), Jim Cahalin, Bill Lally, Joe Kohler, Tom Mullen, Pat Boyle, Bill Pepitone, Joe Wolffe, John Wurm, Harry Voelker, Gene Moore, Fred Mayer, Joe Capizzi, Frank Stangl, Tom Sullivan and others. Many of them went all the way to ordination in 1954 (unfortunately, some left the priesthood later on). Pat Boyle became and is a Trappist monk. Joe Wolffe was one of 17 children (son of a baker in south St. Louis), and John Wurm, who later became an auxiliary bishop of St. Louis and who died of cancer at an early age, was one of 12 children: 17 wolves and 12 worms!! Tom Sullivan later became a Columban Father missionary and served in Korea for many, many years. My classmates were all good fellows, and we had a lot of fun together. The Latin school, located in an old mansion in the middle of St. Louis, did not have classes on Wednesdays but did on Saturdays. The reason for this was to separate us from other young men and in particular from meeting young ladies whose charms might lessen our desire to become celibate priests.

From junior year in high school through 4 years of college, boys aspiring to the diocesan priesthood in St. Louis—headed by the venerable Irish-born John Glennon since 1903 (he was made a cardinal in 1946 and promptly died in Ireland on his way back to St. Louis from the consistory in Rome)—attended St. Louis Preparatory Seminary, at that time under the direction of the Vincentian Fathers. For junior year of high school we were day hops, returning to our homes in the evening. But from senior year of high school through college we boarded at the "Prep." For our senior high and freshman college years we lived in dormitories. For the final three years of college we had roommates. The last two years were devoted to the study of philosophy, at which time the students were robed in cassocks. St. Louis Preparatory Seminary was a bit unique in this arrangement, because at that time in most diocesan seminaries, "minor" seminary ended with the sophomore year of college and students then entered the "major" seminary for six years of study: two of philosophy and four of theology. In St. Louis the "philosophers" at that time were at the Prep, while the "theologians" were at Kenrick Major Seminary. Among the more illustrious "philosophers" at that time going to the Prep, were Bill Mayer, noted for his scholastic achievements—he later became a Trappist monk at the Abbey of Gethsemane—and William Baum, of Kansas City, MO, who later became Archbishop of Washington and Cardinal. Many of my classmates from the Latin School went to the Prep, plus many new students, particularly coming in for the first year of college from high schools, several from St. Louis but others from other dioceses such as Omaha and Nashville.

Among the Vincentians at the Prep in those years, Patrick Mullins taught Greek, and did a pretty good job. He had a wonderful way with words, referring to us as "mental midgets" and urging us to avoid "mental constipation" and "oral diarrhea." I ended up with 4 years of Greek at the Prep, two in high school under Mullins and two in college under Father John Taugher (reading some Platonic dialogues and Homer's *Iliad*). Taugher also taught us Latin—Cicero and Ovid in freshman college and Horace's *Odes* as sophomores. The rector was Father John Zimmerman, a very holy priest and kind leader. Another Father Zimmerman (his first name, I think, was Francis) taught high school Latin. He wasn't the best Latin teacher in the world, but a good priest and a very humble person.

Since I did well academically at the Prep, Archbishop (later Cardinal) Ritter, who had succeeded Cardinal Glennon in 1946, sent me to The Catholic University of America to complete college education. Ritter, it should be noted, immediately desegregated the Catholic schools of the archdiocese. Hence in the fall of 1948 I went to Washington DC to study at CUA and to live with other students for the diocesan priesthood at Theological College, also known as the Sulpician Seminary insofar as it was under the direction of the Sulpician Fathers. I was a Basselin Foundation student in philosophy. Theodore Basselin, who had made his fortune in lumber in upper state New York, had established the Foundation earlier in the 20th century. The program was specifically intended to provide seminarians not only with a good background in philosophy but also in English and public speaking as a way of preparing them to preach. It was a three-year program, leading to the M.A. in philosophy, with special courses in English and public speaking. There were eight of us in the first year program and about 27 students total in the three year program. I had seven classmates: Don Brinley from Indianapolis, Ray Fowerbaugh from Fort Wayne, Leon Meyer, a former marine from Winona, Minnesota, George Kramer from Los Angeles, Tom Mahan from Hartford, Fred Roensch from Milwaukee, and Paul Arbogast from Covington. Of these all except Don Brinley and I were eventually ordained in 1955. Among upper class Basselin students was Raymond Brown, a highly intelligent and amiable person who later became a Sulpician priest and very well known for his work in Scriptural studies, in particular the Johannine literature.

At that time the seminary was so crowded that for our first year four of us—Don, Ray, George and I—shared a room with 2 bunk beds. I was at Theological College (TC) for 3 years of philosophy and one year of theology. All students wore cassocks during the day and for classes at CUA. We wore black suits with Roman collars when we went to the "City," i.e., Washington, D.C.

TC in those days was a wonderful place. A marvelous fraternal spirit animated it—our theme song was "*Ecce quam bonum et quam iucundum, habitare fratres in unum*," ("*Oh how good and wonderful it is to live as brothers who are one."*) The Sulpicians who ran the seminary were, I thought, marvelous. The rector the year I arrived was Father McDonald, known as the "Bunny" for his way of wrinkling his nose like a bunny. He gave marvelous spiritual meditations. Father McDonald had succeeded the beloved Father Anthony Vieban as rector, and Vieban was a hard act to follow since he had a reputation as one of the finest and most saintly seminary rectors around. But McDonald was a worthy successor. I loved him, as did my fellow seminarians. But in the following year he was succeeded by John McCormick, popularly known as "Fat Jack" (he was about 5 feet 2 inches high and approximately as wide). He was a fine priest but quite different in personality from McDonald. My spiritual director was Jules Baisnée, an elderly Frenchman who had lost his left arm during WWI and who taught philosophy, specifically natural theology or what was then called "theodicy," at CUA. Jules was a wonderful, holy man and kind spiritual adviser. But he had a Gallic temper. Since he had only one arm, it was a bit difficult to vest him for Mass, in particular to help him put on the cincture, or rope used to gather the alb. One was supposed to wrap it around him and, when he said, "tie it," to tie it. The problem was that at times one thought, because of his accent, that he had said "tighter" rather than "tie it," and one would pull the cincture tighter around his body. He would then utter a Gallic phrase I cannot repeat, remove the cincture from one's hands, place one end of it in his teeth, and with the one arm/hand whirl it around his body and "tie it." But he was a wonderful, saintly man and good director. After I left the seminary I tried to visit him whenever I was in Washington. In the sixties he became blind and pretty deaf so that it was difficult to get him to recognize who I was. He accepted his sufferings gracefully and died shortly after my family moved to Washington in 1969.

Another holy French Sulpician at the seminary then was Benjamin Marcetteau, a diminutive individual widely respected as an author of spiritual books for seminarians, *The Minor Seminarian* and *The Major Seminarian.*

Basselin students were the youngest in the seminary and low on the totem pole when compared to the "theologians," i.e., those studying theology at CUA. But our older fellow seminarians were a good lot, and kind to us. Among them was Joseph Bernardin, later Cardinal of Chicago, who even then was a marvelous diplomat, a prayerful person, and everyone's friend. Another was John Gavin Nolan, of New York, who later became an auxiliary bishop in the Military Ordinariate and died of cancer at an early age. He was a deacon when I was a first-year Basselin student and was most kind to me. Another was Christopher Huntington, from Huntington, NY. He was older than most and had graduated from Harvard. A convert to the Church, he was a marvelous gentleman, very kind to younger seminarians.

The seminary had rules whose significance I did not understand at the time. I now realize that several of these rules were meant to help students avoid situations when they might be tempted to sexual desires for the same sex. Thus we were told to avoid "particular friendships" and were told to go with those whom we first met during "free periods" and not seek out particular individuals with whom to associate. We were subject to expulsion if we entered the room of other students; the rule stipulated that we "were not to trespass even the sill of the door."

Philosophy at CUA in those days was not as good as it later became. Basselins and other seminarians took most undergraduate courses in Latin—at least from professors who could speak it. Jules Baisnée was one who did, and his course in natural theology was given in a heavily French-accented Latin. Another professor who gave his lectures in Latin was a Franciscan from the Basque country of Spain, Fr. Felix Alluntis, OFM, an authority on the thought of Duns Scotus. Felix taught us logic, metaphysics, epistemology and other philosophical subjects in Latin, with a Spanish/Basque accent, and it was a chore understanding him. He was, however, a very kind and good Franciscan priest, as erudite as can be, and a good philosopher. He later returned to Spain and wrote voluminously on the work of Scotus. Ignatius Smith, O.P., was dean of the School of Philosophy at that time. "Iggie" was a very friendly person and a marvelous orator, who taught graduate courses on the social thought of St. Thomas. I thought his rhetoric more powerful than his philosophical analysis, but I enjoyed his course.

Fulton Sheen was the bright star in philosophy at CUA at that time, and he taught graduate school (where we Basselins joined laymen and women for courses in English). Unfortunately, Sheen retired the year I would have had him—as did the famous psychologist Rudolph Allers—and his successor was not his equal. The very best philosopher at CUA in those years was the Rev. Charles A. Hart, who taught metaphysics. He directed my MA dissertation—on the intellectual cognition of the material singular in the esthetic experience according to St. Thomas—and his graduate courses on St. Thomas were fascinating and communicated to the students a real love of philosophy and some understanding of what it was all about. Some years later I was honored when he sent me an autographed copy of a book he had written on metaphysics, inscribed to "my colleague, William May." Msgr. John K. Ryan taught undergraduate and graduate courses in the history of philosophy in English, not in Latin. We had him for four semesters as undergraduates, and he was an extremely erudite man who spent hours meticulously correcting the many papers he required. I learned much from him and appreciated his courses more later on than I did at the time. My classmates and I found them a bit "boring." We called him "the great dictator" from his habit of dictating notes to correct errors he had discovered in history of philosophy textbooks. I thus chose not to take any of his graduate courses. He was known principally for his wonderful translations of St. Augustine's *Confessions* and St. Francis de Sales' *Introduction to a Devout Life.*

One of the laymen doing graduate work in philosophy whom I got to know was Jude Patrick Dougherty, who later became Dean of the School of Philosophy and did a wonderful job of recruiting good professors so that by the late 20th century the philosophy program at CUA was one of the very best in the country. Jude also proved to be one of my best friends in later life. Getting to know him as a graduate student was truly providential.

During our Basselin years we had special courses in English from Father John Madden. In these classes we focused on the plays of Shakespeare, English literature during in the seventeenth century, and the novels of Thomas Hardy. We also wrote essay after essay for Father Madden's—and fellow classmates'—critique. Msgr. Patrick J. O'Connor of the Savanna-Atlanta diocese, then rector of the National Shrine of the Basilica of the Immaculate Conception, taught us "homiletics" or preaching. He was a real character, impressing on us the need, when speaking in public, to "use our teeth, tongue, lips, and jaws," and to heed the advice Hamlet gave to his players not "to mouth your words." We regularly took turns "orating" before our classmates and Msgr. O'Connor. My favorite Shakespearean discourse was the one from *Hamlet* in which the hero declares: "*O, that this too, too solid flesh would melt, thaw, and resolve itself into a dew.*" I loved to speak this speech because at the time I was overweight by about 40 pounds and my classmates would break into guffaws every time I gave it.

After finishing philosophical studies at CUA I continued there as a seminarian and student of theology. The two most noted theologians on the CUA faculty at that time were Francis Connell, C.SS.R., a moral theologian, and Msgr. Joseph Fenton, a diocesan priest from the Fall River, MA diocese, editor of the *American Ecclesiastical Review,* and professor of fundamental theology and ecclesiology. I never took a course from Father Connell since he did not teach first year students, but I had two courses from Msgr. Fenton. He was an extremely conservative theologian who disagreed vehemently with the more liberal views of John Courtney Murray, S.J. Murray later served as a *peritus* at Vatican Council II, whose Declaration on Religious Liberty (*Dignitatis humanae*) rejected the views championed by Fenton. But Fenton, who also served as a *peritus* at the Council, was a stimulating professor and challenged us in many ways. I found his courses in fundamental theology and ecclesiology fascinating. He early on urged us to read Melchior Cano's *De locis theologicis,* a classic source at that time for fundamental theology and available only in Latin. I got a copy of this famous work, read it, and astounded him when I could summarize its contents. I was his buddy from then on.

I thought that moral theology, taught first year students by a canon lawyer, was incredibly boring. Nonetheless, a paper I wrote for the moral theology course, an analysis of St. Thomas's teaching on the morality of human acts in *Summa theologiae*, 1-2, q. 18, was one that I regarded as the finest I wrote as a student of theology, and I was disappointed that it only merited a B. It was one of the few papers from my student days that I kept. Years later, after I had been teaching moral theology for some time and had studied this difficult and challenging question of the *Summa* (it's one of the longest in the entire work and one of the most difficult) time and time again, I realized that the student paper of which I was so inordinately proud was atrocious. B was too high a grade for it. I then consigned it to the trash.

During first year of theology we also had interesting courses in apologetics and Scripture. We also studied biblical Hebrew. Our Scripture professor, Father John Weisengoff, was very familiar with modern biblical studies and in the forefront of those seeking the renewal of Scripture studies stimulated by Pope Pius XII's encyclical *Divino Afflante Spiritu*. Our Hebrew professor was an unusually erudite Irish-American, Msgr. Martin Higgins. He taught us quite a bit in a year, but unfortunately I soon forgot almost all of the Hebrew that I had learned.

During this year of theological studies I had begun having "dizzy" spells that lasted a short time. During them I would forget where I was and I would always wonder about the time, asking those I encountered "What time is it?" The "spells" did not last long, and were usually preceded by a brief period in which I could, as it were, feel them coming on. They began to occur with greater frequency during the year. One Sunday night, when the second semester was drawing to a close, I experienced one of these "dizzy spells" after Compline, the night prayer. My room was on the same floor as the seminary's rector, Father John McCormick. To go to my room one turned left at the end of the corridor, and to go to the rector's room one turned right. I turned right in my confusion and without knocking simply burst into the rector's room, looked about and asked him "What time is it?" I suppose he gave me the time, so I left and went to my room. The next morning I had a vague recollection of what had happened, so I sought out Father McCormick and he verified that I had indeed burst into his room unexpectedly, looking confused, and had asked him the time. He then had me go to a doctor in Washington for a physical exam. I went through many tests, and the diagnosis was that I was suffering from a "psycho-motor" disorder of some kind and given a medication to help control it. This seems to have satisfied Father McCormick because he allowed me, at the close of the semester, to be "tonsured" and receive what were then known as the first two "minor orders," the first steps to the priesthood, those namely of "porter" and "acolyte."

I returned to St. Louis for the summer, where I worked in the chancery office. Shortly before I was scheduled to return for theological studies, however, Archbishop Ritter had me go through a series of exams at a hospital in St. Louis. I was diagnosed with "petit mal epilepsy." This was bad news indeed, for I then discovered that according to canon law in effect at the time (1952) suffering from epilepsy was a "diriment" impediment to receiving holy orders. I was shocked, to say the least, that canon law at that time included epileptics among the "insane and diabolically possessed," and that as such they were not "fit matter" for ordination to the priesthood. Archbishop Ritter, accordingly, was not able to send me back for further studies leading to the priesthood. He suggested that I remain a seminarian for a spell and teach in the archdiocesan high schools, while we waited to see if medication could effect a cure. I readily agreed to do this. For the academic year of 1952-53, therefore, I taught at DeAndreis High School (co-educational) in north St. Louis. I was assigned the task of teaching American history, world history, and citizenship—subjects about which I knew very little, in fact almost nothing. I had no prior teaching experience. However I accepted the challenge and immersed myself in books on these subjects and did what I could to keep ahead of the class. But a further and very unsettling discovery awaited me. I had always been in schools where my classmates could read and write English, and I was absolutely floored to discover that a good percentage of students at DeAndreis High School lacked these skills. Thus a good part of the year, particularly for one of my classes in American history, taken by *high school juniors* who could not read or write English, was spent in providing a remedial course in reading and writing English, using American history material for sources.

The next school year I was assigned to the newly enlarged DuBourg High School in far south St. Louis. This school was not co-educational since the boys and girls did not attend classes together, but was "co-instructional," since both boys and girls attended but were kept in separate classes. I was assigned to teach freshman and sophomore English and Latin to boys, subjects for which I was better prepared than American and World History. Students at this high school had a better foundation in reading and writing English than those at DeAndreis, but I found maintaining good discipline for the freshmen and sophomore boys I taught was a real problem. For some reason the principal always sent a student of the female persuasion to bring messages to the different classrooms, and whenever a lovely young "co-instructional" female entered the room the boys went crazy. By the end of the first semester I was pretty well down in the dumps. My health had not improved, and it seemed highly unlikely that I would be allowed to continue studying for the priesthood, and I did not think that teaching high school, particularly freshmen and sophomore boys, was meant for me. I thus informed the archdiocese that I was not going to continue as a seminarian and as a teacher in the archdiocesan high school system.

Although I was terribly disappointed that my epileptic condition was a diriment impediment to orders and prevented me from becoming a priest, a goal I had sought since fourth grade some 16 years earlier, I was not embittered or angry. I realized that this was God's will for me and that he had other plans for me. What those plans were was not clear to me at the time, but I knew that he would let me know them as time went by. I believe this news shocked my good mother, who had prayed so hard that her only son would become a priest, more than it did me. My father simply encouraged me to discern some other worthwhile vocation. This condition persisted, although it was controlled by medications, until 1958 or early 1959, when I ceased having any problems and eventually was able to stop taking medication for the condition. During these years of teaching I lived with my parents. My older sister, Rosemary, had married in 1947 and was by then the mother of about six children (she eventually was blessed with seven), and my younger sister, Virginia (Jincey) had entered the Sisters of St. Joseph of Carondelet, and my parents, in particular my father, who was still a Presbyterian, were happy that she seemed to love this life. We had by this time switched from St. Luke's parish to Our Lady of Lourdes, where Msgr. Rogers, the former army chaplain during WW I was pastor, and where the assistant at that time was Father Daniel Moore, an exceptionally holy and intelligent priest who served as my spiritual director.

CHAPTER TWO

Editing Catholic Books

After quitting my high school teaching job and resigning as a seminarian, I first notified my draft board because I had to change my classification from 4D (for "divinity students") to a new one. I was, however, classified 4F because of my medical condition, so I did not have to serve in the army. At that time (1954) we were at peace, so I probably would not have been called up anyway. At first I thought of continuing studies in philosophy at St. Louis University, which at that time had a fine faculty—among them the truly outstanding historian of philosophy James Collins. I thus went to see Father William Wade, S.J., chairman of the department of philosophy. Although he did not discourage me from entering the doctoral program, Father Wade suggested that I first get a master's degree in science, e.g., in physics, so that I could then specialize in the philosophy of science and in that way secure a better paying job after getting a doctorate in philosophy. He also suggested that, if I did not wish to go this route, I should seek work as an editor of Catholic books.

I had no desire to pursue a master's in some area of scientific study, but I found Father Wade's other suggestion intriguing. I immediately began writing letters to well-known Catholic publishers of that day—Bruce, Sheed & Ward, Newman—and to my delight was invited by the Newman Press, then located in Westminster, MD, to come for an interview and an opportunity to join them in an editorial capacity. I went to Westminster, a town some 30 miles from Washington and Baltimore, and had an interview with John McHale, at that time the editor-in-chief of this small company. Newman Press imported and published in the US some outstanding titles published in England and elsewhere, and had begun publishing good American writers. I was hired for the job of assistant editor, which included reading and evaluating manuscripts submitted for publication, copy editing manuscripts accepted for publication, reading galley proofs of books imported from England and elsewhere, and writing blurbs for book jackets. McHale, a former seminarian himself, was a very bright man, with a good knowledge of Catholic theology. He was married and had four children. Tom Schreiber was advertising manager of the firm, and he and his wife Angela became my closest friends in this small town. They later moved to the Washington, D.C. area, and after I had moved there with my family the two families got together. Newman's owner was William Eckenrode, a man who knew how to market books, with a good eye for the Catholic market. He was, however, a bit of a slave driver, as we worked five and a half days a week (Saturday mornings) for very low salaries.

In Westminster I lived in a rooming house, first in an older one near the railway tracks not far from our office (located above the town's movie theatre) and later to a more affluent one further up town, where a number of the local high school teachers lived and where the food, prepared by our landlady Thelma was truly excellent.

Since I had no car, and since we worked half a day on Saturdays, I rarely had the opportunity to go to nearby Washington or Baltimore. I had a lot of time on my hands, and I spent it reading, and reading, and reading, mainly philosophy books and books on Catholic theology. Newman was the American publisher of the superb history of philosophy series by Frederick Copleston, S.J., and I prepared two of those written up to that time for publication in the US. Another terrific book imported from England on which I worked was Bernard Leeming's study of sacramental theology. A short time after I arrived another young man, Clem Anzulewicz, was hired as another assistant editor, and at his suggestion Newman inaugurated a series of anthologies in philosophy, theology, history, and social sciences, the Catholic College Reading Series. Clem contacted US academics to prepare the books on history and social science, whereas I contacted those for books in philosophy and theology. We had a prompt and enthusiastic response and within a short time several volumes that proved quite successful were on the market.

However, I was now over 25 years old, had never been on a date with a girl, and anxious to get married, and to marry a Catholic girl. Unfortunately, there were few Catholic girls in Westminster, MD. I met a few pleasant young women who taught high school, but they were not Catholics and I did not wish to marry any girl who was not a Catholic. In addition, pay at Newman's was very low, and I could see that there was room there for only one senior editor, namely, John McHale, and that he would hold that job as long as he wanted because he was doing a first rate job. There were lots of people who could do what I was doing. Hence I decided to leave Newman and go to Milwaukee, where there was a good chance that the Bruce Publishing Company would hire me. Some years later Eckenrode sold Newman to the Paulist Priests and it became Paulist Press with offices in New York. McHale for a time then served as head editor for the book division of the Pflaum Publishing Company in Dayton, OH. Eckenrode later reentered the publishing arena, this time under the name of Christian Classics, mainly reprints of worthwhile books that had gone out of print. This was located in Westminster. When he died, Eckenrode, in a fine act of remembrance for what he had done, left Christian Classics to McHale, who returned to Westminster with his family after the book-publishing arm of Pflaum folded. John and his wife Kitty suffered the tragic death of one of their boys because of aplastic anemia while living in Dayton, and John, a truly good man, died in the early 1990s.

I went to Milwaukee in July 1955 and was hired by the Bruce Publishing Company as a copywriter in its advertising department, with the promise that, should an opening on its editorial staff occur, I would have first crack. The Bruce Publishing Company was the largest Catholic publishing house in the US at that time. It published around 50 titles a year, many, including novels, for the general "trade," i.e., lay Catholics. Titles included popular works on Catholicism and books of spiritual reading, of which the most popular were by the Trappist, Father Raymond, O.C.S.O., with such titles as *The Man Who*

Got Even with God. Bruce also had a big line of textbooks for Catholic schools from grade school through university, and some sold quite well. There were several series of texts in philosophy, those by Henri Renard, S.J. and Celestine Bittle, O.F.M. Cap. among them, and James Collins' highly regarded *History of Modern European Philosophy.* Bruce also had a list of books in the industrial arts, among them a widely used series of manuals on car repairing. They also published popular prayer books, including a First Communion book in various (and fancy) editions called *Welcome Jesus,* that sold millions annually—one of Bruce's "bread and butter" books.

Bruce was a family-run company, whose president, William C. Bruce, was the bachelor brother of Frank Bruce, deceased. They were the sons of the company's founder, and the original name of the family had been "Bruss," a German name later changed to "Bruce." Frank's sons, William, Frank, and Bob, were officers and managers of the company. William Bruce the younger and nephew of William C., was in charge of production, Frank of sales of "trade" books, and Bob of editorial work on textbooks. A son-in-law, Bob Quinn, was in charge of sales of textbooks. All of them were gentlemen, committed Catholics, family men, and "paternalistic" toward their employees, but in a good sense. The senior "trade book" editor, Al Croft, had been with the company for years. He had been a seminarian and knew Catholic thought very, very well. He was also author of a very popular booklet on the Mass called *The Greatest Prayer: The Mass,* a remarkably fine little book. He was married with a large family. Elizabeth Ewens was in charge of advertising. She was a lively spinster, still living with her elderly mother who lived to be 100 years old, very smart, fun to work for, and very good at her job. We got along fine as she liked my jokes and thought my ad copy, which included writing the blurbs for books, was top-flight. After working in the advertising department for about a year, I was able to join the editorial staff, I worked on both "trade" and "text" books. Al Croft was my mentor as editor of trade books; he was very good to me and helped me enormously with his generosity and advice. Perhaps the most popular "trade" book I ever worked on was *My Other Self* by Clarence Enzler, published about 1956, a remarkable book along the lines of the *Imitation of Christ.* "Clancy" Enzler was an outstanding layman and father of 13 who worked for the

Agriculture Department in Washington. I became good friends with him and his family. After his retirement from the government he became a permanent deacon in the Archdiocese of Washington. One of his sons, John, became a priest and is now Monsignor Enzler, pastor of Blessed Sacrament Parish which serves both the District of Columbia and Chevy Chase, MD. One of his daughters, Kathleen, was a baby-sitter for my family after we moved to the Washington area. Clancy was a true saint, a model Catholic layman, and I pray that one day he will be canonized.

I also worked a lot on textbooks, and here Bob Bruce was my guide. I had to work on some philosophical texts I thought were not particularly good. Among the ones I did not think good was *Man as Man,* a textbook in philosophical ethics by Thomas Higgins, S.J. It sold thousands of copies a year, and I had to prepare a new edition of this work for publication. I thought it legalistic and rationalistic, setting forth an understanding of natural law that I found very unappealing. Other philosophical studies on which I worked, in particular those by Vincent Smith of Notre Dame University on logic, the general science of nature, and the purpose of the school, were very worthwhile. Smith, who later taught at St. John's University in Jamaica NY, died tragically when killed by a drunk driver in Manhattan. He was a fine philosopher and for many years served as editor of the *New Scholasticism,* the journal of the American Catholic Philosophical Association.

Bob Bruce gave me a pretty free hand to search out new authors in philosophy and theology and to develop books that could be used both as textbooks and as general "trade" books for well-educated adults. I had pretty good success in doing this, inaugurating the college theology series of books during and after Vatican Council II under the general editorship of Frank Devine, S.J. and Richard Rousseau, S.J. Of these, some were quite good, e.g., John Powell, S.J.'s *Theology of the Church,* Edmund J. Fortman, S.J.'s anthology of texts on the "theology of God," and some works in biblical theology, among them James Plastaras' *Creation and Covenant.* I also helped work on a new series of philosophical texts under the general editorship of Donald Gallagher of Marquette University. The series Don stimulated included a very important book on metaphysics by Joseph Owens, C.Ss.R. I also persuaded Jude Dougherty, then at

Bellarmine College in Louisville, to serve as general editor of the Horizons in Philosophy series. These were relatively short books on specific philosophical issues; among them were Joseph Owens' *The Meaning of Existence,* and a critique of analytic ethics entitled *Philosophical Analysis and Ethics* by Father Ronald Lawler, O.F.M. Cap. Father Ronald later became one of my very best friends with whom I collaborated on many projects. This saintly priest and scholar died in November 2003. Another fine philosophical work on which I labored was a text in metaphysics by Herman Reith, C.S.C., then chairman of the department of philosophy at Notre Dame University. Father Reith introduced me to a young professor there, Ralph McInerny. I tried without success to get him to write a textbook on the history of philosophy. Now a well-known Catholic philosopher and the author of the Father Dowling mysteries, Ralph is still my friend, although we disagree vigorously on some issues, especially the proper way of understanding natural law.

I also initiated a series of "trade books" for the educated Catholic called the Impact Books series, and one of the first titles in this series was Germain Grisez's *Contraception and Natural Law,* published in 1964. I had been searching for someone to write on this topic. On a visit to Washington, D.C., Father William Wallace, O.P. who had served as editor of the philosophical articles for the *New Catholic Encyclopedia* told me that Grisez, then a young professor at Georgetown University, was working on this matter. I visited him and his wonderful wife Jeannette, and he agreed to let Bruce publish his masterful book, which had been rejected by Doubleday. This was the providential beginning of one of my greatest friendships. When I read Germain's wonderful text I discovered why I had not liked Thomas Higgins' presentation of natural law (*Man as Man*). It is what Germain identified as "conventional natural law theory," one found in many neo-Scholastic texts. Although adherents of this theory, like Higgins, cited St. Thomas time and time again, they were reading him through the lens of the famous seventeenth Jesuit scholar, Francis Suarez, whose understanding of natural law is indeed legalistic and rationalistic.

Among other books in this series were Dietrich von Hildebrand's *What Is Philosophy?,* George Montague's *Maturing in Christ: St. Paul's Program for Christian Growth*, and Raymond Brown's *Does the*

New Testament Call Jesus God?. As a result of the success of these works, by the end of the 1960s I had acquired a reputation in Catholic publishing circles as a leading editor, and in fact was offered a job by the more prestigious Catholic publishing firm of Sheed & Ward, whose senior editor was the highly regarded Catholic intellectual Phil Sharper. Sharper was a former Jesuit seminarian, who had shaped some of John Courtney Murray's essays into the highly influential work *We Hold These Truths*.

MARRIAGE

But I am getting ahead of myself. Milwaukee was also a very *Catholic* city, and there were many good Catholic girls around. There were several who worked at Bruce, and I began to date them. I was living in a boarding house near the border of the City of Milwaukee and the suburb of Shorewood, WI. My housemates were mainly medical and dental students from Marquette University, although one, Jude Hoepper, who remains a friend, was in the graduate business school. My parish was St. Robert's in Shorewood (home parish of Bob Bruce, his wife Pat, and family). I had no car, so when I took girls out for dates we used pubic transportation. I usually took them to dinner and a movie or a play or the Milwaukee Symphony. I dated several young ladies from Bruce. They were all very fine and intelligent persons, and devoted Catholics. I finally mustered enough courage to kiss one of them, Doreen Ackeret, a Marquette U graduate working as an editorial assistant on one of the magazines that Bruce published. I walked on air afterwards.

But there were other fine young Catholic ladies in Milwaukee, particularly among the nurses at St. Mary's Hospital, which was not far from my boarding house, and at Marquette University— particularly in the nursing school at St. Joseph's Hospital. From 1955-57 I dated many, and my heart went out to several—all of them wonderful Catholic young women who were chaste and let me know it. On Friday December 13, 1957 God's providence led me to attend a pre-Christmas dance sponsored by Catholic Alumni of Milwaukee, a group of graduates, male and female, from Catholic colleges throughout the US. I took a St. Mary's Hospital nurse to the affair, Roxanne by name—a very attractive and fine young woman. But at the dance I met a truly marvelous and beautiful nurse, Patricia Ann Keck, from St. Louis. Pat had obtained her master's in nursing science from St. Louis University in 1956 and had come to Milwaukee to teach pediatric nursing at Marquette University's School of Nursing. When we discovered that we both hailed from St. Louis our interest in each other picked up. As a child she had lived in the Cathedral Parish of St. Louis, where Father Charles Helmsing (my former Latin school teacher) was assistant, and she had loved him as I had. I was smitten! After I had taken Roxanne home I knew I would never go out with any other girl than Pat Keck.

During the next few weeks we met every week, frequently attending daily Mass at the Gesù Church of Marquette. By the end of January 1958 I was sure I wanted her to be my wife. We both wanted to have a large family. I thus proposed to her by the end of January, a few short weeks after meeting her, and she accepted!!! My heart overflowed with joy. We delayed a bit in informing our parents of our decision to marry, but we did so early in the year. We arranged to visit her family, then living in Mt. Vernon, IL, and mine, still in St. Louis, around Easter time. Since we were adults they could not really oppose our marrying, and they quickly came to realize why we had both made good choices. Her parents, Leonard and Lucille Keck, were wonderful people. Len was a salesman at the time for Standard Brands, and Lucille was a good cook, seamstress, and homemaker. Pat was an only child; a younger brother had died in infancy, but she had numerous cousins and longed to have a bunch of children. My parents immediately loved Pat and were enthusiastic about our wedding. My father had retired from the Standard Oil Company that year, but he had acquired a realtor's license and was specializing in commercial real estate. He was still not a Catholic, and I was surprised at that, as I thought he had refrained from becoming a Catholic because of his mother's somewhat hostile attitude toward the Church. However, she had died in 1948 and he had not entered the Church. He later became a Catholic when he was 75 years old, in 1968, and you can imagine the joy that brought to my mother, my sisters Rosemary and Jincey, at that time Sister Robert Mary, C.S.J. of the Sisters of St. Joseph of Carondelet—although at that time she may have changed her religious name to Sister Virginia—she was then teaching French at Avila College in Kansas City MO.

Pat and I were married in St. Mary's Church in Mt. Vernon, IL on October 4, 1958, the feast of St. Francis of Assisi, and this was undoubtedly one of the greatest days in my life and a gift from God's providence, for she is a very holy and good woman, and has been a real source of Christian love and support for me since then.

DOCTORAL STUDIES

In 1959 Marquette University began offering a doctorate in philosophy again. Since I was still very interested in philosophy and had been working on many manuscripts and books dealing with philosophy I decided, with Pat's encouragement, to pursue the possibility of entering the doctoral program at Marquette and continue working as editor at Bruce. When I discussed the matter with Bob Bruce, he was very enthusiastic. So much so that he persuaded the management at Bruce to give me time off to take a course or two a semester and during summer school—and also *to cover the cost of the courses.* How generous!!!! I thus began taking doctoral level courses at Marquette in the fall of 1959, and I continued taking courses (one or two a semester and during summer school) through 1961. After passing the comprehensive exams in 1962 I began work on my doctoral dissertation, a study of the reality of matter in the metaphysics of Henri Bergson. Because I was also working a very full schedule, and because I became discouraged about finishing it at times, it was not until early 1968 that I finally finished the study and successfully defended it. Had Pat—and the Bruces—not encouraged me to keep at the dissertation I would never have finished it. It was good that I did so, because by gaining my Ph.D. in 1968 I received my "union card" for obtaining a decent position in academe, even though I did not think, at the time, that I would ever leave the publishing field.

The graduate philosophy department at Marquette was very good. Perhaps its leading luminary was Gerard Smith, S.J., author of excellent works in metaphysics and the philosophy of God. Lottie Kenzierski taught very good courses on Aristotle and St. Thomas, Beatrice Zedler good courses on contemporary philosophy and American philosophy, Charles J. O'Neil very fine courses on Aristotle's ethics, Michael Murray, S.J., good courses on Ockham, Bergson, and

Aquinas. But the professor who really made me work was William Donovan, S.J., whom we all called "Wild Bill" Donovan. He was the old-style Jesuit, who worked his students like crazy. He taught courses on Plato and Plotinus, and for them we had to read the original Greek texts. It was something, and by the time I had taken three of his courses I was able to read those texts pretty well. Another fine professor was Francis Wade, S.J., brother of the William Wade of St. Louis. I did not, however, have the opportunity to study under him. He later served as chairman of my dissertation committee after Father Murray, who was my director and first chairman of the committee, died of brain cancer.

The year I received my doctorate, 1968, is notable for two events, one deeply affecting the Catholic world, the other dramatically affecting Bruce employees. I will soon get to these, but first I want to say a few words about our family life and a third notable event of 1968, the birth of one of our daughters.

Pat and I wanted a large family, and God blessed us with many children—eventually a total of seven. While we were living in Milwaukee's suburb of Whitefish Bay, he blessed us with Michael William (1959), Mary Patricia (1960), Thomas Robert (1962), Timothy Patrick (1965), Patrick Joseph (1966), and Susan Marie (1968). Pat had quit working outside the home and devoted herself to the care of the children. When Michael was a few years old I read a fascinating book by Nancy Rambusch on Montessori education, *Learning How To Learn*. I told Pat she had to read it, and she did. Shortly afterwards she and several other young mothers formed a club and took a correspondence course in Montessori from the St. Nicholas Training Centre in London, and they invited teachers from that Centre to come in two summers to offer formal classes. We purchased a good deal of the educational equipment used in the Montessori method, and Pat did a wonderful job of educating our children in this method at home (we could not afford to send them to the Montessori schools). Later on, after our move to Washington, Pat took two years of formal courses in Montessori education at the Washington Montessori Institute, receiving certificates for teaching Montessori to children from ages 3 through 12. Still later—in the 1990s—she took summer courses given in Denver, CO for teaching Montessori to children from birth through 3 years of age, and for one year she taught 2 year old children in a Montessori school near our home. Later in the 1990s and early 2000s she became very involved in the Catechesis of the Good Shepherd, a Montessori-based program developed by Sofia Cavaletti. She did so in order to help in the religious education of our grandchildren. Now back to the two events of 1968.

The major event of 1968 deeply affecting the Catholic world was the publication in July 1968 of Pope Paul VI's encyclical *Humanae vitae,* in which he reaffirmed the teaching of the Church on the intrinsic immorality of contraception. Recall now that I had looked for and succeeded in finding an author, Germain Grisez, who had written a book on contraception and natural law to show how reasonable and true this teaching of the Church is. Recall too that Pat and I wanted a large family and at the time the encyclical was issued we were anticipating with joy Susie's birth. Obviously Pat and I did not practice contraception, and we had no intention of doing so. However, during the debates over contraception from 1964-67, I began to waver in my conviction that contraception is intrinsically immoral, thinking that some arguments advanced by Catholic theologians, especially that set forth in the so-called "Majority Papers" of the Papal commission on the subject, to justify it had some plausibility. But most of all, during those years I was very proud and wanted very much to be counted among the *illuminati,* the bold, courageous thinkers in Roman Catholicism. I wanted this particularly because I was aggressively seeking new authors and new books reflecting the "theology of the future." Hence, when *Humanae vitae* was published and a significant number of these "bold, courageous thinkers" signed a document dissenting from it, I accepted the invitation to join the signatories. I had some guilt feelings about doing so because deep down I still thought that there was something very wrong with contraception. I would never have practiced contraception, and had I even thought of doing so, Pat would have thrown me out of the house. I realized that my decision to sign the dissenting statement was motivated, in large measure by base, vainglorious considerations—which were quickly rewarded when Justus George Lawler named me an associate editor of *Continuum,* a journal "on the frontiers" of theology, noted for its "advanced" views. At Newman I had worked on a very interesting book by Lawler, a professor at Xavier College in Chicago, on the Christian imagination, and on another book of his after I joined Bruce. I did not tell many people that I had signed the dissent; I did not, for instance, tell my wife. When she learned that I had, she did not say a word, but her look of utter contempt spoke volumes. Signing this document, however, proved providential, for doing so helped me land the job of teaching moral theology at The Catholic University a few years later!

The other notable event of 1968, particularly for Bruce employees, was the sale of the family-owned firm to the giant publisher Macmillan. When the sale was made, the new owners deliberately misled the employees, including the Bruces, assuring all that the company would remain in Milwaukee, that few jobs would be lost, and that editorial direction would not change. Soon, however, we learned that the big printing plant that was part of the operation would close. I was informed that the entire operation would be closed down and was offered a chance to move to New York and continue working as an editor. I did not accept this offer, as I was utterly disgusted by the way Macmillan had misled my fellow employees. I immediately began search for another editorial position.

Of course, an event of importance for our family during this year was the birth of our daughter Susan on October 5, the day after our tenth wedding anniversary. I remember that during the delivery of our baby, Pat's wonderful Catholic doctor, John Brennan (a pioneer in "natural childbirth" and NFP), and I were discussing the "new techniques of reproduction" such as *in vitro* fertilization then being promoted in books like Gordon Rattray Taylor's recently published *The Biological Timebomb* and how dehumanizing such techniques of "making babies" are.

I was fortunate in that Corpus Instrumentorum, a publishing arm of the World Book Company, had been started a few years before by a group, mainly of priests, who had been heavily involved in the preparation and publication of the *New Catholic Encyclopedia*. These priests, academics for the most part, had succeeded in convincing the World Book Company that there was need for scholarly works in Catholic thought, and indeed, for an English language version of an encyclopedic work of Catholic theology of the caliber of the famed *Dictionnaire de théologie catholique*. Corpus Instrumentorum was the subsidiary World created in our nation's capital to achieve this goal, and it had already given contracts to noted authorities throughout the world to contribute book-length articles for the projected new encyclopedia, with the idea of publishing at least some of them as books prior to completion of the encyclopedia itself. In addition, there were to be other general "trade" books for the educated Catholic laity and for use in colleges and universities. The president of Corpus was the Rev. John Whalen, who had been a student at Theological College a few years ahead of me and who served also as acting president of The Catholic University of America in the wake of the turmoil caused by dissent over *Humanae vitae* from 1968-70. Father Whalen fortunately had need for another book editor at the time. He offered me the job toward the end of 1968 (Bruce would close down at the end of that year).

Thus, in February 1969, my family and I moved from Milwaukee (Whitefish Bay actually) to Kensington, MD, a suburb of Washington, D.C. Prior to moving there, Pat and I, with baby Susan, had made a trip to the area to find a home. Jude Dougherty, then dean of the School of Philosophy at CUA, was most helpful in aiding us find a very nice one near Holy Redeemer Church and School. We had hoped to spend one night in a hotel after driving from Milwaukee to the DC area and then take possession of our new home, but we were not able to do so. The Doughertys insisted that our entire family—at that time Pat and I and six children—stay in their home until we could move into our own. What generous friends.

I thus began working as an editor for Corpus Instrumentorum in February 1969. Among the books that I developed at Corpus was *Hello, Lovers! An Invitation to Situation Ethics* by Joseph Fletcher and Thomas Wassmer, S.J. Fletcher, at that time professor of Christian Ethics at the Episcopal Theological School in Cambridge, MA, was the celebrated author of the 1965 highly influential *Situation Ethics*. Fletcher championed the view that love is the only absolute and that intentionally killing innocent persons, committing adultery or fornicaton or what have you can at times be the "loving thing" to do. I had known Wassmer, a Jesuit moral philosopher who taught at St. Peter's College in Jersey City. He was then on a sabbatical and working with Fletcher at the Episcopal Theological School. I tape recorded a long discussion by the two on

"Christian ethics." Since Wassmer, to my surprise, sang the same song as Fletcher, I was obliged to offer objections to their "situationism,"—actually a pseudo-Christian version of utilitarianism. Thus the book, which was published with Fletcher and Wassmer as authors and me as editor, turned into a three-way dialogue. I affirmed that there are specific moral norms that are absolute and can never be violated because the actions they forbid are "intrinsically evil." I said, for instance, that it is always morally evil intentionally to barbecue a baby. The Vietnam War was going on at the time and Fletcher claimed that if Ho Chi Minh were willing to end the war if I would barbecue a baby before his eyes, I would be morally obliged to do so, for this would be the most loving act in the situation and would save many other babies from being barbecued by napalm. Wassmer heartily agreed with Fletcher. I found their situationism, which is actually a crude variant of the "proportionalist" method in moral theology then regnant among many Catholic theologians, utterly repugnant. Fletcher frequently voiced vigorous opposition to the thought of Paul Ramsey, a Methodist who taught Christian ethics at Princeton University. I had not, at the time, read anything by Ramsey, but I resolved to read him. If Fletcher didn't like him, he must be good— and he was!!! I wanted the jacket of the book to show Fletcher and Wassmer standing at an altar and robed in priestly garments, offering a barbecued baby to Moloch. My superiors at Corpus, however, would not allow this for the jacket.

Among the new titles for which a contract had been made was a magnificent book on abortion by Germain Grisez. Germain, who undoubtedly was very distressed that I had signed the dissent from *Humanae vitae,* kept his counsel to himself on this matter and let me serve as the one to prepare this marvelous study for publication. It was over 600 pages in length, a work of immense scholarship, and it examined the issue of abortion from the medical, scientific, legal, historical, religious, sociological, and moral perspectives in great depth. In it Germain further developed the natural law theory, rooted in the thought of Thomas Aquinas, that he had outlined in his 1964 *Contraception and the Natural Law.* This book, *Abortion: The Myths, the Realities, and the Arguments,* was published in 1970, three years before Roe v. Wade, and it remains one of the very finest works on this subject. In it Germain brilliantly showed the fallacious reasoning used by many writers, including Catholic moral philosophers and theologians, to justify the intentional killing of the unborn, and in doing so made it luminously clear that the reasoning used to reach this conclusion was the same kind of reasoning used by the same authors a few years earlier to justify contraception. By divine providence I was able to work on this magnificent study which helped me see how terribly flawed was the moral theory used to justify contraception. This theory led to the kind of ethics championed by Fletcher and Wassmer. I was repentant of my cowardice in signing the dissent to *Humanae vitae*, but I did nothing publicly to retract my views. Nor did I talk to my wife about the matter or to anyone else for that matter.

Grisez had finished his manuscript by the fall of 1969 and it could have been published early in 1970. There was, however, a delay in its publication caused in part by problems at Corpus Instrumentorum and its relationship with the parent World Publishing Company. Corpus was spending a lot of money and many of the book-length manuscripts intended for the encyclopedia and independent publication were either very slow in arriving or else, on completion by the authors, judged not worth publishing (by editors like me and some outside readers) either because they did not meet the scholarly standards expected or because in their present state they required extensive rewriting in order to make them intelligible. My own suspicion is that some of the manuscripts, allegedly written by world-famous academics, had in fact been composed by their graduate assistants. As a result of all this, World Publishing decided in June, 1970 to close Corpus's offices in Washington. I was, however, retained as editor and instructed to move to New York, NY with my family and to work from the corporate office there. My superior would be William Yeomans, S.J., an English Jesuit whom Father Whalen had hired some months previously as an editor. I did not wish to move my family from our home in Kensington, where we had lived only a year and a half, and I also suspected that my future was not too secure. I thought that mine was pretty much a "salvaging" operation, to go over the several book-length manuscripts that had been under contract as major articles in the projected encyclopedia and to recommend some for publication and others for the circular file. I was surprised to find Father Yeomans my boss. I had thought him a close friend after he arrived in Washington, and I was somewhat in awe of him as he seemed so much more knowledgeable about contemporary theology than I. He was not in favor of publishing Grisez's masterful but lengthy work on abortion because he thought that the massive volume on abortion by Daniel Callahan and published by Macmillan early in 1970 was the best "Catholic" work on the subject—Callahan argued for the morality and legalization of abortion in some cases—and when the index of over 50 pages for Grisez's book was prepared Yeomans tried to prevent its publication. Fortunately, he was not successful.

A substantial sum of money had been put aside to pay for moving expenses from Washington to New York, and I used this money to cover the cost of traveling weekly to and from. I would leave home early on Monday morning and take the early shuttle flight to LaGuardia airport and return by train on Friday afternoons. During the week I lived at a hotel near our office and worked during the day, sorting out what I judged to be publishable manuscripts from those not worth publishing. Among the publishable ones were the fine work on apologetics by Avery Dulles, S.J., a study of the development of dogma by the Belgian Dominican Jan Walgrave, O.P., and a brilliant study of existentialism by the noted Scotch theologian John Macquarrie, plus Grisez's superb work.

The months (mid June through December 1970) that I commuted weekly from our Kensington home to Manhattan were very hard for my family. Our youngest daughter, Susie, 20 months old when this began, would look under the bed and in closets for me on Monday morning, and from the time I arrived home on Friday evenings until bedtime Sunday would cling to me as much as possible. It was, of course, very hard for Pat to care for our lively six children without me to be of any help at all for five days of the week.

As I anticipated, I was told shortly before Christmas 1970 that my services would not be required in the new year. I was now the unemployed father of six children, and I learned, on telling Pat of this news, that God was blessing us with another baby, whose expected delivery would occur in August 1971.

Fortunately, Corpus had arranged a good contract with World, providing its key employees with six months' severance pay, and I was, fortunately, making a decent salary at that time. Finding another job, however, was very difficult. I sent out more than 800 resumes and soon discovered that there were absolutely no openings in editorial work among publishers willing to publish the kind of books I was qualified to edit intelligently or find authors willing and able to write them. I applied for all kind of jobs in the federal government—the largest employer in the DC area—and I obtained a high civil service rating so that, if I could find a post in one or another federal agency I would be paid rather well.

A great opportunity arose when Russell Shaw, a journalist friend who collaborated closely with Germain Grisez in some writing projects, and well known in Catholic circles, recommended me to Patrick Cardinal O'Boyle for the job of his press officer. I visited the great Cardinal O'Boyle in his office on a Friday, and at the end of the interview he offered me the job, telling me to report for duty the following Monday. I was overjoyed. However, on Saturday Cardinal O'Boyle, outstanding for his defense of Pope Paul VI's *Humanae vitae* and for his keen sense of social justice (he desegregated archdiocesan schools immediately on becoming archbishop in 1948), called me at home to tell me that he had reconsidered matters and that he was not going to give me the post. I was crushed, but I realized that the reason he had changed his mind was that he undoubtedly had discovered that I had signed the dissent from *Humanae vitae* in 1968 and I had not publicly retracted my dissent (I had not brought the subject up for discussion when he interviewed me). My friend Germain Grisez later informed me that Cardinal O'Boyle asked him about me and, since I had not publicly retracted by dissent from *Humanae vitae,* that he did not recommend me.

Another opportunity arose when the editorship of the Catholic magazine *Marriage,* published by St. Meinrad's Abbey in southern Indiana, opened up. I went to St. Meinrad's for an interview and was offered the job. However, the largest "city" in the area was Jasper IN, a town of some 10,000 people. I had been a big city boy all my life and I had difficulty seeing how my family and I would do in this rural setting. Moreover, the magazine itself was in a slump, and there was the possibility that it might cease publication in a year or so if its economic condition did not improve (and as things turned out, it did). Moreover, at that time there was a live possibility that I would finally land a job with the Social Security Administration. Those who had interviewed me on a few occasions had told me that I was their first choice for the job, but that it would take time for red tape to be untangled. Hence I had no job, and more than six months had passed. My father, who had helped us out before in emergencies, generously came to our aid, helping me to meet mortgage payments and other bills, and we also began to benefit from the food stamp program. But if a job were not found soon, it would be necessary to sell our home in order to survive.

Then, in God's providence, I was given the opportunity to enter academic life and to teach moral theology.

Toward the end of July my friend Jude Dougherty told me that there was an opening in moral theology or "Christian ethics" in the Department of Religion and Religious Education at CUA. Daniel Maguire, a priest from the archdiocese of Philadelphia, had determined to leave the priesthood and to marry one of his graduate students. But according to the rules in effect at CUA any priest who sought to leave the priesthood and to marry could no longer teach at the University. Maguire, a highly popular professor, took legal action to prevent this, but he was not successful, and as a result the Department needed someone right away to teach his courses, insofar as the school year would begin in less than two months. Maguire succeeded in finding employment immediately in the theology department of Marquette University, where he is still teaching and writing books and essays defending contraception, abortion, and euthanasia.

Alerted to the opening available at CUA, I immediately applied for it. I was well known to several of the faculty members, including Maguire, because of my publishing activities and also because of the active part I had taken in the College Theology Society, originally known as the Society of Catholic College Teachers of Sacred Doctrine. I had also published a book, *Christ and Contemporary Thought*, in 1970 that had been well received. They all knew that I had signed the statement dissenting from *Humanae vitae,* as had Maguire and others, including their colleague in the School of Theology at CUA, Charles Curran. The Department's committee for appointments and promotions voted to recommend me for the position, the faculty voted to accept me, and the dean of the graduate school, of which the Department of Religion and Religious

Education at that time was a part, approved of the appointment. I now had a new job, assistant professor of Christian ethics (moral theology) at The Catholic University of America. I am certain that one of the reasons why I was judged the right person for the job was the fact that I had signed the dissent from *Humanae vitae,* whose principal author was Charles Curran. The issue was not discussed during the interviews, nor did I let anyone know that I was now sorry that I had signed the document. I am most grateful to the senior members of the department of religion and religious education—Berard Marthaler, OFM., Conv., chairman, William Cenkner, O.P., Sister Mary Charles Brice, O.S.B., and others for giving me the opportunity to enter academic life, right after the time, August 4, 1971, that our seventh child, Kathleen Ann, was born.

Salaries at CUA, especially for assistant professors, were pretty low, and my salary from the University at that time was almost 40 percent lower than the salary I had been receiving. Fortunately, Father Harry Flynn, rector of Mt. St. Mary's Seminary in Emmitsburg, MD, had invited me to give a seminar to his students once a week, early on Monday mornings, and the money from this part-time job was a great help. Moreover, the Department of Religion and Religious Education offered courses during the "minimester" between graduation and commencement of summer session, and also during summer sessions. I would thus be able to earn an extra two months' pay by teaching minimester and summer school. But now I had to prepare for teaching "Christian ethics."

CHAPTER THREE

TEACHING MORAL THEOLOGY

The best way to learn a subject is to teach it, and I now had the serious responsibility to teach moral theology. Fortunately, I had taken good courses at Marquette on St. Thomas, including his moral thought, and the great advantage of having worked with Germain Grisez. His marvelous books on contraception and abortion set forth a moral theory rooted in the thought of St. Thomas that not only showed me that the kind of natural law theory found in the manuals of moral theology and some standard philosophical textbooks allegedly based on St. Thomas were in fact Suarezian in nature, rationalistic and legalistic, but also that the moral reasoning used to justify contraception led to the denial of all specific moral absolutes. I learned much, too, from some ethical writings of John Macquarrie and from the excellent and provocative work, *What Is Ethics All About?*, which Corpus had published, by the British Dominican Herbert McCabe, O.P. (its title in England was *Law, Love, and Language*). I also found the writings of Paul Ramsey, a Methodist who was professor of Christian Ethics at Princeton University, of extraordinary help. Ramsey, whom the situation ethicist Joseph Fletcher, as we have seen, vehemently disliked, was a wonderful opponent of situation ethics and other trends in Protestant thought. These trends denied the existence of moral absolutes (that is, specific moral norms such as those prohibiting the intentional killing of innocent human persons.

Ramsey was a strong defender of the inviolable right of innocent human persons, including unborn children, from direct attack upon their lives. He also was very open to Catholic natural law theory and had followed carefully the teaching of Vatican Council II on moral issues, far more faithfully than most "Catholic" thinkers. He, Grisez, and John Finnis of Oxford University in England were undoubtedly the most articulate and cogent defenders of the existence of moral absolutes and, corresponding to them, intrinsically evil acts, in the English-speaking world. The great majority of Protestant authors and of influential Catholic theologians (e.g., Charles Curran, Richard McCormick, S.J., Joseph Fuchs, S.J., Louis Janssens, head of moral theology at the prestigious Louvain University) all denied that there are any specific moral norms that are absolute, i.e., without exceptions; they claimed that one could rightly choose to kill an innocent person or have intercourse with someone not one's spouse, etc., provided this was necessary either to secure a "higher [premoral] good" or avoid a "greater [premoral] evil." They all had adopted some form of "proportionalism" or "consequentialism," i.e., the claim that one could determine, prior to choice, which alternative promised the greater good or lesser evil, and that one ought then to choose that alternative. They thus attached an "exception-making" criterion to *every* specific moral norm. Thus they held that "it is morally wrong to kill an innocent human person, or it is morally wrong to have intercourse with someone other than your spouse, *unless doing so is necessary to achieve some greater good or avoid some greater evil.*"

Grisez's work, as noted, had shown me that this kind of moral reasoning was precisely the same as that underlying the acceptance of contraception by Catholic theologians. Those who used it to justify contraception in the late 1960s may not have first realized how truly revolutionary it was and that it inevitably led to the acceptance of abortion, non-marital sex, homosexual acts, or whatever behavior one might consider. However, by the mid 1970s this was clearly recognized, as Charles Curran frankly acknowledged in one of his essays (e.g., "Divorce from the Perspective of a Revised Moral Theology," in his book *Ongoing Revision in Moral Theology*).

In December 1971, during the semester break of my first year teaching at CUA, I met Paul Ramsey at a meeting in Washington of the American Academy for the Advancement of Science, which that year was focusing on the issue of *in vitro* fertilization. Among speakers at the meeting were Robert Steptoe, the British doctor who pioneered the technology of "test-tube" babies and who in 1978 succeeded in bringing to birth Louise Brown, the first human conceived *in vitro* to survive until birth, Daniel Callahan, founder of the Hastings Center, and Paul Ramsey, who delivered a powerful address to show the intrinsic evil of generating human life in this way. I later taught a doctoral seminar at CUA on Ramsey's massive work. This giant in the field of Christian ethics died in 1987.

Among others attending the conference was Father John Harvey, O.S.F.S., who at that time taught moral theology at DeSales School of Theology in Washington. He was some 10 years older than I, but we became fast friends; he is today one of my closest friends and a true friend of my whole family. In many ways he reminds me of the saintly Father "Mac" of St. Luke's Parish during my boyhood. In my view John Harvey is a living saint; he is the founder of Courage, an organization dedicated to helping persons who find themselves sexually attracted to persons of the same sex to live lives of perfect chastity.

At CUA I was teaching two sessions of a course on introductory moral thought to undergraduates and a graduate course on contemporary moral thought. I now saw that the reasoning supporting contraception was the proportionalistic understanding of human acts that inevitably led to acceptance of killing innocent persons, etc.—a view confirmed by the "Notes in Moral Theology" by Richard McCormick, S.J. in the March 1972 issue of *Theological Studies*. In this article McCormick hails the advance in moral thought made by those who deny that there are *any* kinds of human actions, described in non-morally evaluative language, that are *always immoral*. Nonetheless, during my first year of teaching I was so cowardly that I did not speak out in the classroom against contraception, although I did defend the existence of moral absolutes, for instance, the norm prohibiting always and everywhere the intentional killing of innocent human beings, against the proportionalists. I simply avoided the issue of contraception and focused on that of abortion when I turned to specific issues.

However, by my second year of teaching I realized that I simply had to teach my students that contraception is intrinsically evil and give them good reasons to show why. Consequently, I began doing so and also tried to show that contraception was the gateway to abortion and that the reasoning justifying it inevitably led to the denial of all moral absolutes. I had also initiated new courses for undergraduates on bioethics and the just war theory. I worked very hard during my first two years to write articles for scholarly publications, and was successful in having several accepted. Hence at the end of my second year of teaching and the end and my first two-year contract, I was not only given another two-year contract but also promoted to the rank of associate professor. I thought I was on my way to a tenured position in the Department of Religion and Religious Education.

However, when my next two-year contract expired in 1974, I was told that I would not be rehired. I was not given the reason for this decision, but I am morally certain that I was fired because of my position on contraception; I know that some students had complained about my views on this issue to the chairman of the Department. I was crushed. I now had to search for other employment.

I was offered a position at Loyola University of the South, in New Orleans, and, more fortuitously, the offer to teach moral theology in the Archdiocese of New Orleans' seminary by Archbishop Philip Hannan, and as an added inducement Archbishop Hannan promised that our family could live, rent free, in the former bishop's residence across the street from the seminary. It was a mansion with some 7 bedrooms and a living room the size of a small ballroom. Archbishop Hannan also offered to take care of the college expenses of our children (a key benefit of CUA employees was tuition-free education at the University for children if they met the admissions requirements). I undoubtedly would have accepted this generous offer from Archbishop Hannan had not Father Carl Peter, then chairman of the Department of Theology at CUA, invited me to apply for an opening in moral theology in his faculty. At that time, the most prominent member of his faculty was Father Charles E. Curran [In a reorganization at CUA shortly after I became a faculty member in 1971, the Department of Religion and Religious Education, which had been part of the Graduate School, became one of the departments in the newly established School of Religious

Studies, and the old Schools of Theology and of Canon Law were reduced from Schools to departments in this newly formed school.]

By now, it was known that I supported *Humanae vitae*—this was one of the principal reasons why Father Peter wanted me in his Department, for he wanted me to teach the courses on marriage and sexual morality. I was delighted to apply and was accepted by the faculty, including Father Curran, as a new member. In two years time I would complete six years of teaching at CUA and, if I did not secure tenure by then, would be told to leave and seek employment elsewhere. I worked very hard those two years, teaching courses on Catholic sexual ethics and marriage to students in the M.A. and M.Div. programs, courses on the value of human life, the morality of lying and other issues to those in the licentiate (STL) program, and courses on the ethics of Paul Ramsey and natural law in the Catholic tradition to students in the doctoral (Ph.D. or STD) programs. I published many, many articles and two books. I came up for tenure review in 1977. Fortunately, and providentially, Father Carl Peter, who was then Dean of the School of Religious Studies, broke the tie vote of 3 for and 3 against given by the departmental committee for appointments and promotions. I believe, but cannot prove, that the three faculty members who voted to give me tenure were Father Patrick Granfield, Father William Hill, O.P., and Father Avery Dulles, S.J., and I am most grateful to them. The fact that Paul Ramsey, who had been one of the "external" readers, asked to evaluate my work, and thought it good, was a big help. Father Curran, known as "Charlie" by everyone, told me that he had voted against me because he did not think that I was "pastoral" enough in my approach, particularly in teaching seminarians.

Prior to obtaining tenure, I had worked as the theological consultant to a group of bishops preparing a pastoral letter on the moral life. The Most Rev. John McDowell, auxiliary bishop of Pittsburgh, was the chairman of the committee. Russell Shaw, who at that time was the media spokesman for the United States Catholic Conference, and Germain Grisez had both recommended me to Bishop McDowell for this position. The committee had prepared a draft of the proposed pastoral letter and sent it to some 800 Catholic scholars, members of different professional bodies such as the Catholic Theological Society of America, the American Catholic

Philosophical Association, the Catholic Historical Association, etc., asking for advice and reaction to the draft document. One of my responsibilities was to read every response received, summarize its contents and give Bishop McDowell, who then personally read each response, my opinion of its value. Many of the more widely known theologians either chose not to respond at all or else wrote to say that they would give advice only if the bishops guaranteed their willingness to accept it!!! In the early 1970s the bishops had asked theologians for their advice in preparing a revised edition of their *Ethical and Religious Directives for Catholic Health Facilities*, and they did not accept the advice of those who thought that Catholic facilities could and should provide, for instance, contraceptive sterilization. In fact, after this document was published Richard McCormick S.J. wrote an essay commenting on it in the Jesuit weekly, *America*, entitled "Not What the Doctor Ordered." Since the bishops obviously could not guarantee these theologians that their advice would be accepted, they simply did not offer any. Some other theologians submitted essays denying moral absolutes and proposing the proportionalist method of making good moral judgments (for example, one theologian sent the committee a copy of Louis Janssens's celebrated "Observations on *Humanae Vitae*" from the 1969 volume of *Louvain Studies*, an essay in which he attacks the encyclical and claims that both Vatican Council II and St. Thomas Aquinas deny moral absolutes and urged the committee to follow his method of making moral judgments). One of the most helpful submissions by a theologian came from Paul Quay, S.J., who taught physics and theology at St. Louis University and who later wrote an important essay criticizing proportionalism. The response from the philosophical community was much better. By far the most helpful commentary and critique of the draft document came from Germain Grisez, who time and again sent in sound advice to the committee.

  I recall a meeting of the committee in Cincinnati at the home of then auxiliary bishop Daniel Pilarcyzk, when there was reluctance on the part of some of its members about even mentioning the issue of contraception in the proposed Pastoral. I asked the assembled bishops whether they believed this teaching to be true. When they said that they did, I said to them, "Then go ahead and tell the faithful."

There was subsequently an effort, engineered by highly placed ecclesiastics in the bureaucracy of the then United States Catholic Conference, to "submarine" the Pastoral. In fact, an alternative draft was commissioned by some officials and produced by a theologian teaching at Notre Dame University. It was what I call a "milquetoast document". It had some lovely things to say about the Catholic moral life as a "sharing" of the gift of oneself in love to others in ever-enlarging concentric circles, beginning with one's family, one's parish and neighborhood, and extending to the civil society and indeed to the global society. This alternative version, however, did not contain one "no." It said nothing about the kinds of actions the Church regards as intrinsically evil, for instance, adultery, the intentional killing of the unborn, and contraception. Fortunately, the Committee, under the leadership of its chairman Bishop McDowell, rejected the alternative version and finally secured the Bishops Conference's approval of the Pastoral, entitled *To Live in Christ Jesus: A Pastoral Reflection on the Moral Life.* It was published in 1976. Thanks to the willingness of the Committee to speak the truth, this pastoral letter, which Pope John Paul II publicly praised during his first apostolic visit to the United States in October, 1979, explicitly reaffirmed the Church's teaching on the intrinsic immorality of contraception. It also did a good job of portraying Catholic moral life, not as a set of legalistic impositions arbitrarily imposed on men and women to inhibit their freedom, but as truths meant to help them make good moral choices so that they could follow Christ and share in his redemptive work. It was a great honor to work on this document.

Bishop McDowell and the bishops on the committee, among them the then Bishop of Cleveland who later became the Cardinal Archbishop of Washington, James Hickey, recognized the very significant help given them by Germain Grisez, so much so that some of them secured the funds to establish the Flynn professorship of Christian Ethics at Mt. St. Mary's Seminary precisely so that Grisez could have this as a home base for his work in moral theology. The professorship was named after the seminary's former rector, Harry Flynn, now the Archbishop of St. Paul.

Through the providence of God I had become a tenured professor at CUA. I was becoming well known as a defender of

Humanae vitae and, with Grisez, Joseph Boyle, John Finnis and others, as an opponent of the proportionalist method of making moral judgments championed by such "giants" in Catholic thought as McCormick, author of the extremely influential "Notes on Moral Theology" that appeared every March in *Theological Studies,* and the other theologians named earlier. I also led the fight against a very bad book commissioned by the Catholic Theological Society of America and published in 1977, *Human Sexuality: New Directions in American Catholic Thought,* edited by Anthony Kosnik, Agnes Cunningham, Ronald Modras, James Schulte, and William Carroll, and published by the Paulist Press, a book later censured by the Congregation for the Doctrine of the Faith.

1978 is for me a most memorable year for many reasons. First of all, it was during this year the Fellowship of Catholic Scholars held its first annual meeting in Kansas City, MO. The Fellowship had been founded the year before by a group of Catholic scholars led by Msgr. George A. Kelly, Father Ronald Lawler, OFM Cap., James Hitchcock, Germain Grisez and others. Its statement of purpose declared: "We Catholic scholars in various disciplines join in fellowship in order to serve Jesus Christ better by helping one another in our work and by putting our abilities more fully at the service of the Catholic Church." The members of the Fellowship, this statement continued, "wholeheartedly accept and support the renewal of the Church of Christ undertaken by Pope John XXIII, shaped by Vatican II, and carried on by Pope Paul VI…and accept willingly in faith the defined teaching of the Catholic Church and those teachings taught by the Church's ordinary and universal magisterium, and we acknowledge also our duty to adhere with religious assent to those teachings which are authoritatively even though not infallibly proposed by the Church." Although I was not one of the founding members of the Fellowship, I joined it as soon as I heard of its existence.

A fellowship of this kind was providential at that time because dissent from magisterial teaching was not only widespread but also almost *de rigueur* on Catholic campuses. The Fellowship offered Catholics faithful to the magisterium and marginalized in their own institutions great support. Msgr. Kelly, who died in 2004, was its founding father, and Lawler its first president, and both of these great priest-scholars, in particular, Father Lawler, have truly been gifts of God's providence to me, for they have helped me out in so many ways. I later served as president of this wonderful organization in the late 1980s. It is now over a quarter-century old and growing in strength.

1978 was also the year that Seabury Press published Timothy O'Connell's *Principles for a Catholic Moral Life*. Widely praised by Fuchs, Curran, and other "revisionist" theologians, this was the first textbook in moral theology specifically written for use in Catholic seminaries, colleges, and universities, that integrated the proportionalist method of making moral judgments. Earlier in the year Grisez had seen William Cardinal Baum of Washington to ask him to sponsor a conference on moral theology to deal with dissent in fundamental moral. Baum was willing to sponsor such a conference at CUA. When O'Connell's book appeared, I went with Grisez to see Cardinal Baum (whom I had known when we were both students at St. Louis Preparatory Seminary) and he told us to go ahead and make preparations for a week-long conference at The Catholic University of America on moral theology. The conference itself was not held until June, 1979.

With the help of others, in particular Father Lawler, we organized a group of Catholic scholars faithful to the magisterium to present papers at this conference, and prepared papers of our own. Among the speakers were John Finnis of Oxford University, Rev. William Smith of St. Joseph's Seminary in New York, Father Lawler, Joseph Boyle, and Louis Bouyer, a famous French theologian. Cardinal Baum himself gave a fine paper. The conference was well attended, and the papers given at it were published under my editorship as *Principles of Catholic Moral Life* in 1980 by Franciscan Herald Press. It took up the same issues treated by O'Connell and offered an incisive critique of proportionalist moral thought and the radical notion of "fundamental option" associated with that methodology that falsely relocated self-determination from the free choices we make every day to an alleged act of core or basic freedom at the center of our existence. It was at this conference that I first met John Finnis, whose work I so much admired. John contributed a splendid essay on natural law in the documents of Vatican Council II. Father Lawler, with whom I have had the privilege of collaborating on different projects, contributed a fine paper on mortal sin, and Joseph Boyle, who had studied under Grisez at Georgetown University, a magnificent critique of fundamental option theory. Joe became one of my best friends, and we have worked on several projects together.

1978 is memorable also because it marked the tenth anniversary of *Humanae vitae*. I recall an incident involving a colleague in the Department of Theology at that time, Father William Shea. He had come to CUA from St. Joseph's Seminary in Dunwoodie, N.Y., and he made it known that he did wish to return to Dunwoodie. One day in the hallway as the encyclical's anniversary was approaching, he elbowed me and said, with a mischievous grin, "The Pope is not our only hope." Those words ran through my mind the whole day and night, and the next morning I composed a poem to commemorate the event and gave the poem to Shea as a gift at Christmas. The poem follows:

The Ballad of William Shea

"The Pope is not our only hope," said the Rev. Dr. Shea.
"We've Charlie Curran and Avery D. right here at CUA.
With others too to search for truth, including Dr. May.
No need to fear that grand barque, the Church on Peter found,
Will be submerged in treacherous seas with folks like these around."
"Good Lord," exclaimed his Eminence, on hearing of Shea's hope,
"This poor deluded maniac's setting up an anti-Pope!
Off with his head, out with his tongue! This nonsense we must end,
and in support of Christ's dear Pope, troops rally to defend!
The rack, the screw, and burning fire, while quick and sure are dire.
In charity these cannot be fit tools of righteous ire.
Yet what to do to bring an end to madness such as this,
And save our flocks from errors that imperil heavenly bliss?"
I know not how this tale begun shall come upon its end.
Perhaps poor Shea, untenuréd, to Dunwoodie will go.
In exile there to end his days, in sorrow and in woe.

The following year Shea left the priesthood, married a former nun, and began teaching at the University of South Florida. He later became chairman of the Department of Theology at St. Louis University.

At the end of June, 1978 and first week of July I was at a conference sponsored by the Human Life Center at St. John's University in Collegeville, MN. By this time I was well known for my support of *Humanae vitae,* but I had never publicly acknowledged that I had signed the dissent from this encyclical nor had I publicly repented of it. Patrick Riley, at that time editor of the *National Catholic Register* and preparing an issue to celebrate the encyclical's tenth anniversary, was shocked to discover my name among the dissenters. He phoned me at the Human Life Center Conference to find out why I had signed the dissent and what had caused me to change my mind. I sent him a written response, summarizing what I have already said here about the matter, and he published my retraction in the July 2, 1978 edition of his paper. This marked the beginning of another of my greatest friendships. Pat is a man of great courage and principle, resigning his job at the *Register* some time later when its publisher at that time wanted the paper to air the opinions of dissenting theologians. Prior to the publication of *Humanae vitae,* Pat had published a wonderful two-part article, "The Wholeness of Marriage," in the May and June 1968 issues of *Homiletic and Pastoral Review.* In this remarkable article, which I discovered only in the 1990s, he offers a wonderful criticism of the dualism and consequentialism underlying the apologia for contraception set forth in the so-called "Majority Papers" of the papal commission on the regulation of birth, the argument that I (in 1967 when it was made public) had found somewhat persuasive.

In July 1978, to mark the 10th anniversary of *Humanae vitae,* the Department of Religion and Religious Education at CUA and the University Chaplain announced that they would sponsor a talk on the encyclical, whose anniversary is July 25th, by Father Curran. I phoned the Chaplain and said I could understand why he wanted Father Curran to speak on the issue, but I said that I would like to have the opportunity to respond to him. The Chaplain told me that this could not be arranged, but that he would announce, at the beginning of Curran's lecture, that he was sponsoring a talk by me on contraception and *Humanae vitae* the following week. On the night of the lecture, however, as I was walking into the auditorium where Charlie was going to speak (it was crowded with at least 300 people) the Chaplain stopped me and said that he had to withdraw his invitation for me to speak the following week. I asked him why, and he said that Father Curran had told him that, if he made this announcement, he (Father Curran) would refuse to speak under his auspices, although he would give the talk he had ready. The Chaplain told me that this would be "too embarrassing." After the lecture I stopped Charlie and said that I was surprised that he, noted as he was for advocating free speech in the Church, had prevented me from speaking. Charlie replied that it was the Chaplain, not he, who was preventing me from speaking. He told me that if the Chaplain announced his sponsorship of a talk by me on this subject the following week, this would have given the audience the impression that what he (Charlie) was going to say that evening was "not Catholic teaching." I replied that I thought that what he said that evening was indeed *not* Catholic teaching. Although Father Curran was (and undoubtedly still is) a warm and friendly person, he certainly knew how to play "hardball."

When Father Peter, dean of the School of Religious Studies, and Father John Ford, C.S.C., chairman of the Department of Theology, learned what had happened, they were upset and promised that they would sponsor a talk by me on *Humanae vitae*, but that it could not be arranged until the fall. They kept their word, and I thus gave a public lecture at CUA that fall defending *Humanae vitae*. I want to note here that Father Ford, a great Newman scholar, was a superb departmental chairman, scrupulously fair and just in his relations with the faculty. Father John Ford, C.S.C., is not to be confused with Father John C. Ford, S.J., a Jesuit who was at one time a professor of moral theology at CUA and a staunch defender of *Humanae vitae*.

Another memorable date in 1978 occurred on July 25, when Louise Brown was born, the first child conceived *in vitro* to survive the petri dish and the womb to be born. In the mysterious ways of divine providence, this child was born precisely 10 years later to the day after *Humanae vitae* was signed, the great encyclical in which Paul VI had declared: "there is an inseparable connection, willed by God, that it is not lawful for man to break on his own initiative, between the unitive and the procreative meanings of the conjugal act." Contraception severs this connection by intentionally setting aside the procreative meaning of the conjugal act; *in vitro* fertilization and other reproductive technologies that manufacture life in the laboratory are even more radical, transforming the generation of human life from an act of *procreation* into one of *reproduction*. But in many ways contraception paved the way for all this, because contraception in effect sunders the bond between sexual behavior and the generation of human life.

A final memorable event of this most memorable year, 1978, was the election, on October 16, of Karol Wojtyla as the new Bishop of Rome, Pope John Paul II, whom divine providence elevated to the papacy to raise his voice vigorously during the final years of the 20th century and the early years of the 21st in defense of the inviolable dignity of human life and of marriage, the God-given "rock" on which the family is built, the sanctuary of life and love.

By the mid 1980s, having published several books and scores of essays, I was fairly well known in the field of moral theology. During this time Pat was busy with her studies of Montessori, and she also did graduate studies at CUA in nursing science, obtaining her doctorate in nursing science in 1989. Her original goal was to resume teaching pediatric nursing and integrate Montessori ideas into the curriculum. Unfortunately, she was not able to realize this and has since spent her time doing Montessori when possible with our grandchildren in the Washington area. She has also become very interested in the Catechesis of the Good Shepherd, a religious education program pioneered by Sofia Cavalletti, which integrates the principles of Montessori education into the catechetical formation of children.

Because I had a pretty good record of publications and my classes seemed to be going well, I applied for promotion from associate professor to full or ordinary professor. I did so three times in the early 80s; the first two times I was not successful and was told by some on the relevant committee (which included Father Curran) that my writings were "too polemical," i.e., too critical of theologians such as McCormick, Fuchs, and their like. Finally, on the third attempt in 1985 I had success when some who opposed me abstained and I received one vote sufficient to win this promotion and, with it, a decent increase in salary. Salaries at CUA were then, as they probably are now, lower than those at other academic institutions because of the great dependence of this fine university on tuitions for income.

I had been asked to stop teaching at Mt. St. Mary's Seminary after I entered the Department of Theology in 1975, and since this department, unlike the Department of Religion and Religious Education, offered no courses during the minimester or summer school that avenue of income had disappeared. However, in 1975 I began teaching "upper school" religion at the superb St. Anselm's Abbey School near CUA. My oldest son Michael was a student there (at that time it was open to boys from seventh grade through high school, and Michael entered when he was in eighth grade). I had class at the Abbey School Monday, Wednesday, and Friday early in the morning and I then went to CUA for my classes there. All four of my sons—Michael, Thomas, Timothy, and Patrick—attended this great school, and I enjoyed teaching there from 1975 until 1989. The income was used to help offset the cost of tuition, and my sons also worked hard to contribute their bit to their education, as did their sisters—Mary Pat, Susie, and Kathleen—who attended the Country Day School of the Sacred Heart, Stone Ridge, in walking distance of our home. Tuition for our children in these schools was considerable, despite the assistance generously offered lower-income families.

Among the students I had at the Abbey School was Peter Casarella, a good friend of my son Tom. Peter later earned his doctorate in theology at Yale University and now teaches at CUA. I think that one of the courses he took from me at the Abbey School, which I called "Readings in Christian Classics," got him interested in pursuing the study of theology. This course included Augustine's *Confessions*, the prayers and meditations of St. Anselm, selections from St. Bonaventure and St. Thomas, and Chesterton's *The Everlasting Man*. He has a well-earned reputation as one of the finest young theologians of the day. I am very grateful to the Benedictine Monks of St. Anselm's Abbey and School for giving me the chance to teach there and of being so good to my family. I am in particular debt to Fathers Michael Hall and Peter Weigand and Abbot Aidan Shea.

When they entered college four of my children—Michael, Timothy, Patrick, and Susie—took advantage of the great fringe benefit CUA employees enjoyed of tuition-free education at the University for their children, while three—Mary Pat, Tom, and Kathy—chose to do their undergraduate work at Harvard, Yale, and Duke Universities respectively because of pretty good financial assistance and scholarships. Tim attended the University of Chicago as an undergraduate for two years, but then decided to finish at CUA.

My father, who had become a Catholic when he was 75, died at age 82 on December 1, 1975, after a year in which he had been bedridden after a fall and injury to his head. My mother generously offered some financial assistance to us during these years, and Pat's father, a wonderful man who had by this time achieved remarkable success as a financial planner gave us substantial help at times of crisis. He also gave wonderful care to his wife Lucille, who began suffering from Alzheimer's disease in the early 1970s and died a year after my father did. Lucille could, for some reason, remember who I was and who my parents were. She thought I had a lovely wife and beautiful children, but she did not realize that my wife was her own daughter and my children were her grandchildren!

"Grandpa" Keck continued to live in Mt. Vernon, IL, but he visited us regularly. Our children loved him dearly. He would take them on long walks and frequently say the rosary with them during these walks. He had come to stay with us for several months when he died at age 89 of congestive heart failure in our home in January 1994, after spending Christmas holidays with us. My mother had died of pancreatic cancer in July 1985. She had been diagnosed with this form of cancer early in the year. I was planning to fly to St. Louis with my youngest daughters Susie and Kathy to visit her in August when my sisters Rosemary and Jincey called to tell me I had better come home immediately if I wanted to see her before she died. I got to St. Louis on a Friday and was getting ready to return home on that Sunday, July 20, 1987, when my mother, who was mentally alert and rejoiced in having me with her, suddenly died. Divine providence had brought me home in time to be with her at the time of her death, and by his providence both my sisters were with her too.

In 1985 Grisez and I were among a group of Catholic moral theologians from around the world who met at the Universidad de Navarra in Pamplona, Spain, to plan an international congress on moral theology to be held in Rome in 1986 and to be co-sponsored by the John Paul II Institute for Studies on Marriage and Family in Rome, under the presidency of Msgr. Carlo Caffarra, and the Collegio Accademico della Santa Croce, also in Rome and sponsored by the prelature of Opus Dei. Our preparatory meeting, held at Opus Dei's university in Spain, gave me the opportunity to meet fine European theologians, among them Ramón García de Haro, an Opus Dei priest from Barcelona who was teaching at the John Paul II Institute in Rome.

Ramón and I soon became very close friends. Upon returning home I would write him in Spanish, and he would write me in English—if my Spanish was as hilarious as his English, the correspondence was really something. I recall at one time he told me that some name was on "the point of his tongue." Since Ramón taught in Rome, I was able to see him frequently in the next decade because of trips there, and in large measure it was through his friendship with me that I finally realized I had a vocation to Opus Dei, which I joined as a supernumerary member in 1991. Ramón, an outstanding moral theologian, died of lung cancer in 1995. It was his death that finally convinced me to stop smoking.

The Congress for which we prepared in 1985 centered on the theme, "The Person, the Truth, and Morality." It was held at the Lateran University in Rome where the John Paul Institute was housed in March 1986. It was a great success and was followed by a second international congress in 1988 to mark the 20th anniversary of *Humanae Vitae*. Carlo Caffarra, who was then the president of the John Paul II Institute for Studies on Marriage and Family in Rome, became a good friend. He was named Archbishop of Ferrarra-Comachio in 1995 and, around Christmas of 2003 Archbishop of Bologna. Caffarra is a profound thinker and wonderful gentleman who speaks Italian clearly and beautifully. His *Living in Christ Jesus* is a marvelous account of Christian morality. This wonderful man was made a cardinal by Benedict XVI March 24, 2006.

In 1986 our Holy Father, Pope John Paul II, appointed me to the International Theological Commission, which was under the direction of the Congregation for the Doctrine of the Faith, of which Joseph Cardinal Ratzinger was head. This was a group of 30 theologians from around the world, which Pope Paul VI established after Vatican Council II. It met annually in Rome and members served for a five-year period and were eligible to serve longer. John Finnis and I were the first laypersons chosen to serve on this body. During the first year of the five-year period, the group selects four topics for study for the next four years, and frequently different Vatican congregations propose issues that they wish considered. Subcommittees are then formed to study the topics chosen and to prepare drafts of documents for consideration and debate by the entire group at the annual meeting, usually held the first week in October (except for years when a Synod of Bishops is being held, and then the meetings are held in December).

When I was a member we lived and met at the Casa Internazionale del Clero (now renamed the Domus Pauli Sexti) in the historical center of Rome near the Piazza Navona and in walking distance of the Vatican. Many priests who work in different Vatican offices live in this beautiful building, and clergy from around the world can stay there at a reasonable price when visiting Rome if space is available. I think that Finnis and I were the only laymen who were allowed to live there. We had our meals there, and I remember the time when fruit was served for dessert and I took an apple and began to eat it the way we do in the good old USA by putting it to my mouth and sinking my teeth into it. My tablemates looked at me with horror!!! What a barbarian!!! I was told to use the "coltello," the knife, and to cut it up into small pieces and then use the fork to transfer them from the plate to my mouth.

I was a member of this body for 10 years. During the first five years in addition to Finnis other members of the Commission were Carlo Caffarra, the friendly and theologically profound president of the John Paul II Institute for Studies on Marriage and Family in Rome, and my CUA colleague and friend, Father Carl Peter, who had been on the Commission for some years. Father Peter and a few other members spoke Latin fluently and would at times give their papers or comments in that language. Bonaventure Kloppenburg, a German-born Franciscan who taught theology in Brazil, must have learned Latin at his mother's womb, as he spoke it as easily as I speak English and would frequently crack jokes in it as well. Commission members were allowed to speak in Italian, English, French, Spanish, and German, and three magnificent translators would immediately provide fairly accurate renditions in each of these languages for the others. One of the translators, Leo Elders, S.V.D., a Dutch priest and noted Thomistic philosopher, had been a missionary in Japan, and I think he could speak 12 or 15 languages fluently. A remarkable man! During the second five years that I was on the Commission Father Peter, who had died tragically and suddenly of a heart attack, was replaced by Avery (now Cardinal) Dulles, S.J., who by then had retired from CUA and was serving as university professor at Fordham University.

There were two high points during the week's meetings: the first was the honor of being invited to participate at the Holy Father's private Mass early in the morning on one of the days and to meet briefly with him afterwards; the second was a delicious "pranzo" for the commission hosted by Cardinal Ratzinger during the week. Ratzinger, who presided at the deliberations of the Commission, impressed all of us with his great gentleness, inward tranquility, and ability to speak German, Latin, French, Italian and English beautifully. He tried to attend all the sessions, and on the final day of the meeting, a Saturday, he would deliver a marvelous theological reflection, in Latin, on the theme that had been discussed.

In 1988, the 30th anniversary of our wedding, Pat accompanied me to Rome. That year I could not live at the Casa del Clero since women were not permitted to live there, so we resided at a nearby hotel. Pat, however, was invited to come with us to the Holy Father's private Mass. That was the year John Paul II's Apostolic Letter *Mulieris dignitatem* had been issued, and I had picked up a copy at a Vatican bookstore early in the week. The day before we met with the Holy Father Pat had attended a Mass in St. Peter's celebrated by him, and she had a copy of the beautiful little missals printed on such occasions. I asked Cardinal Ratzinger whether I might ask the Holy Father to autograph my copy of *Mulieris dignitatem* and he said to go ahead. I did so and the Pope graciously signed my copy with his autograph, *Joannes Paulus PM* (Pontifex Maximus) *II*. It is a treasured reminder of that wonderful meeting. Pat asked if he would sign the missal she had from the previous day's Mass, and in it he wrote: *JP PM II*! Cardinal Ratzinger kindly invited Pat to the "pranzo" he hosted for the members of the Commission, giving her a seat of honor next to him and a beautiful bouquet of flowers to commemorate our 30th anniversary.

One year the Holy Father invited members of the Commission to have lunch with him, and we went in two different groups on two different days. How wonderful this was. Cardinal

Ratzinger made sure that each one of us had an opportunity to say something to the Holy Father during the meal. At its conclusion, Pope John Paul II stopped Carlo Caffarra and me, and asked Msgr. Caffarra about the new session of the John Paul II Institute that had opened in Washington, D.C. Caffarra said that it was off to a good start. The Holy Father then poked me in the chest with his index finger and said, "You must help this Institute!" I replied that since I was teaching at The Catholic University of America, I did not see how I could. He then said, "You will find a way."

In September, 1987 Archbishop (later Cardinal) Jan Schotte called me from Rome to say that Pope John Paul II had appointed me a "peritus" for the forthcoming Synod of Bishops to be held in October on the theme: The Mission and Role of the Lay Faithful in the Church. [During this year the International Theological Commission would meet in December.] Since classes had already begun at CUA I said I could not do this, but Schotte said I could and must. Fortunately, the day before he called, I had lunched with Daniel Mindling, a Capuchin priest who had just finished his doctorate at Oxford under John Finnis. Father Mindling did not have a teaching position as yet, and he was the perfect one to take over my classes at CUA for the month of October when I would be in Rome for this Synod. God's providence took care of a real problem.

Hence I spent the month of October 1987 in Rome at the Synod, and during this month I again was housed at the Casa del Clero, where many of the Synod Fathers also resided. There were sixteen of us "periti," among them Joseph Fessio, S.J. I discovered that we had a lot of work to do. Each one of us was assigned some key themes to track in the speeches given by the Synod Fathers during the first week of the Synod, and each day we had to rush to our quarters at the noon break and summarize the themes assigned to us. We then went to the Synod Hall an hour before the afternoon sessions were to begin and orally communicated to the Cardinal "Relator" of the Synod our summary findings and turned in our written summaries. After the afternoon (4 p.m.-7p.m.) session ended and after supper, we had to prepare summaries of what had been said to hand in the next morning.

That weekend we broke into four groups of four periti each and prepared a draft of the "Relatio" that Cardinal Hyacinthe

Thiandoum of Dakar, the "Cardinal Relator" of the Synod, would present to the entire Synod the following Monday, summarizing what the individual Synod Fathers had said about the mission and role of the laity the week before. The Synod fathers then broke into "language groups" for debates and discussion of the "Relatio." There were two English language groups, from A to M and from M to Z. I was in the M to Z group. My job was to listen and to speak only when asked to clarify some theological point, and I was rarely asked to speak. Hence for the most part I simply listened.

Among the "auditors," i.e., lay persons invited to participate in the sessions but without votes, was Jan Vanier of Canada, founder of the Arche movement to establish centers to care for mentally handicapped persons. He gave several beautiful and inspiring addresses to the Synod Fathers in our group.

At the end of the "language sessions" the Synod Fathers prepared a draft document with some 54 propositions regarding the role of the lay faithful in the Church. These propositions were then debated in the language sessions and various "modi" were proposed. During the final weekend of the Synod, six groups of "periti", each under the direction of 3 Synod fathers, had the task of considering each "modus" to determine which ought to be integrated into the draft text and which ought not (giving a reason why the proposed modification was not accepted)and then prepare a final draft. Each group had 9 propositions with their modi to consider. It was a lot of work, and our group had the advantage of being under direction of Archbishop Derek Worlock, of Liverpool England, a veteran of other Synods. Worlock had the reputation of being a "liberal"; he was a hard worker and I enjoyed working with him. After the Synod Fathers had approved the amended version of the original text, some journalists covering the Synod said that some Fathers thought that the Holy See had exercised pressure behind the scenes to secure some modifications in the text. Worlock, an honest man, publicly declared that of the Synods in which he had participated this was the most open and that this tale of Vatican pressure was scurrilous.

During the Synod the Holy Father would sit patiently during the time when the Synod Fathers were giving their papers, listening carefully. He met with different groups of bishops and others for breakfast, lunch, and dinner, and on one occasion honored the "periti" by inviting them to dinner at his table. I sat near him during the meal, in which the conversation focused on his recent apostolic visit to the United States and on some of the themes of the Synod. He was most gracious as our host. I said very little because both because I was in such awe and also because I experienced problems in swallowing because of a hiatal hernia.

I continued teaching at CUA and in the summers of 1989 and 1990 took part in workshops sponsored by the recently established section of the John Paul II Institute for Studies on Marriage and the Family in Washington, D.C. The Department of Theology at CUA, unfortunately, looked at the new Institute with some hostility—the very name evoked outrage from some—as did some other departments within the School of Religious Studies. There was one meeting at which the new Institute was discussed, and the majority of the faculty spoke disparagingly about it. Father Robert Sokolowski, of the School of Philosophy (an "ecclesiastical school" since it offered pontifical degrees) and I were the only two present who defended the new Institute as a true academic body. I could do so because I had tenure, fortunately. At the close of the meeting, I said to one of my colleagues, a theologian faithful to the magisterium but who at that time was not tenured and therefore kept quiet during the meeting, that there was great "opposition" to the Institute. My colleague replied, "Opposition? It was venomous hatred." This colleague, Robin Darling Young, later obtained tenure at CUA and a reputation as an authority on the Syriac Fathers of the Church. In 2003 she transferred from CUA to Notre Dame University.

The School of Philosophy, under Jude Dougherty, was cooperating with the Institute, and Father Sokolowski offered courses open to both John Paul II Institute students and CUA students. In the spring of 1991 Carl Anderson, Vice President and Dean of the Washington session of the John Paul II Institute for Studies on Marriage and Family, invited me to offer a course that could, like Sokolowski's, be taken by both CUA and John Paul II students. I accordingly proposed a course of this kind to my department chairman (unfortunately Father John Ford no longer held that post) and to the dean of the School of Religious Studies (again, unfortunately, Carl Peter was no longer its dean since he had died of a massive heart attack a short time earlier). When my superiors rejected this proposal, I was angry. I had been teaching at CUA for twenty years, the veteran of many academic wars at this truly fine University, the kind of wars that occur not infrequently in the groves of academe.

When I told Anderson that my superiors would not allow me to teach a course for both CUA and JPII students, he offered me a full-time position on his faculty. I thought the matter over and took counsel with James Cardinal Hickey, whom I admired greatly as one of the greatest, if not *the* greatest bishop, in America. Cardinal Hickey, a man of great humor and kindness, was also a firm supporter of the Holy Father and did what he could to make The Catholic University of America a place where magisterial teaching was honored. He thus had stood firm when the "Curran" controversy arose in the late 1980s and supported the judgment of the Congregation for the Faith that Father Curran could no longer be regarded as a Catholic theologian because of his dissent from Catholic teaching. Curran fought this decision in the courts, but lost. He was, however, only the tip of the iceberg, and the majority of the theological faculty at that time supported him—in fact, I recall that in a vote taken by the faculty of the Department of Theology which in effect was a vote for Curran or for John Paul II, 17 or so votes were for Curran, and only 4 were for John Paul II. At a later meeting of the Catholic Theological Society of America the vote was approximately 320 for Curran, 14 for the pope!

Cardinal Hickey did something to stop dissenting theologians from teaching at CUA *if* there was a "smoking gun," e.g., a book or article clearly repudiating Catholic teaching. For example, when the faculty had granted tenure to a moral theologian, Father John Dedek, from Chicago, I took some books of Dedek's to then Archbishop Hickey, showing him relevant sections that he should read. He did so, and then called Cardinal Bernardin of Chicago, Dedek's ordinary, to say that, as Chancellor of the University, he did not want Dedek teaching at CUA; in order to teach at the University Dedek needed Bernardin's permission. Cardinal Bernardin then made Father Dedek a pastor of a parish in the Archdiocese of Chicago, and to his credit Dedek was silent about this event and never afterwards wrote on moral issues until his death a few years ago. Hickey also blocked the appointment of Rev. John Boyle, who had been teaching theology at the University of Iowa for years, as dean of the School of Religious

Studies. The faculties of the departments of this School had elected him Dean and the President of the University, at that time Father Joseph Byron, S.J., was ready to announce his appointment. I took Boyle's book, *The Sterilization Controversy*, to Archbishop Hickey. He read this book, which rejected Church teaching on contraception and contraceptive sterilization, and called Father Boyle in to see him. Hickey told Boyle that if he accepted the position he (Archbishop Hickey) would be obliged in conscience to fight the appointment and that it would be a nasty fight. He thus asked Father Boyle to remove himself from consideration for the post, which he did.

It was because I respected Cardinal Hickey so greatly that I wanted to see him before deciding whether to leave my tenured position at CUA for the untenured but very promising position at the JPII Institute. I was inclined to make the change because I was by then battle weary and also attracted by the larger salary promised to me. Cardinal Hickey, who was Vice Chancellor of the Institute and a firm supporter of it, was also the Chancellor of CUA. Being determined to make CUA more "catholic," he, in many ways, would have liked me to stay on CUA and continue in efforts to help the University and its students remain faithful to magisterial teaching. But Cardinal Hickey could see good reasons for my leaving. He told me to make up my own mind and that he would support me. Cardinal Hickey was a true friend. He is a man of remarkable humility and humor, and I want to illustrate his humor with an anecdote.

The late pastor of my home parish, Msgr. Leo Coady, had been a student at Theological College with Cardinal Hickey in the late 1940s just before I arrived to study philosophy. Coady was a year ahead of him, and was in charge of the seminary choir. At Msgr. Coady's funeral, Cardinal Hickey gave a brief talk at the end of the Mass and said that when he was ordained a deacon, he was worried about singing the "Ite, missa est" at the end of high Masses. Coady told him that it was the same tune as the "Kyrie, eleison." However, Cardinal Hickey continued, when the Mass ended instead of singing "Ite, missa est," he sang "Kyrie, eleison." Naturally, everyone laughed. A year later there was a memorial service at the Shrine of the Immaculate Conception for Father Walter Schmitz, S.S. who had been in charge of liturgy at Theological College when both Coady and Hickey were seminarians. Hickey told the same story, only this time it was Father Schmitz, and not Coady, who told him to sing the "Ite, missa est" to the tune of "Kyrie, eleison," and again everyone laughed. After Mass I said to His Eminence, "Cardinal, that's a great story. But tell me, who was it who told you how to sing the 'Ite, missa est.' Was it Coady or Schmitz?" Without missing a beat, Cardinal Hickey replied, with a twinkle in his eye, "They both did." A great story.

I chose to leave CUA and become the Michael J. McGivney professor of moral theology at the John Paul II Institute for Studies on Marriage and Family, beginning with the fall semester, 1991. The professorship was named after the great priest, now being considered for canonization, who founded the Knights of Columbus in the nineteenth century. The Knights of Columbus provide the financial support for the Institute.

Despite some academic wars during my years at CUA, I am grateful divine providence gave me the chance to teach there. I had many wonderful students, including seminarians. When I first began teaching there in the early 1970s the common attitude among seminarians was a "hermeneutic of suspicion", i.e., "if the Church teaches something, it's probably wrong." However, the situation had changed considerably by the end of the 1980s, and thanks in part to the work of John Paul II, there was a much greater openness to magisterial teaching. I retain friendships with many of my students. I also respected my colleagues on the faculty, even when we had serious disagreements. Father Curran and I were friendly to each other when we served on the same faculty, and he is a kind man— the sort who will give his shirt off his back to help someone in need. Many of my CUA colleagues, for example, Father Patrick Granfield, Avery (now Cardinal) Dulles, John Ford CSC, Joseph Jensen, OSB, Father Christopher Begg, are my friends today, and I can never forget Carl Peter's support when I joined his faculty. Carl died tragically of a sudden heart attack in the early 1990s. I had good friends with many from other faculties, for instance Fathers Robert Sokolowski, John Wippel, and Kurt Pritzl, OP, of the School of Philosophy, and of course their Dean, Jude Dougherty, Father Robert Trisco of the Church History Department, Charles Dechert from Political Science, Leopold May of the Chemistry Department, and many others. I am happy that a very fine young theologian, John Grabowski, was the person chosen by the faculty (including me at the time) to take my position on the faculty. Since my departure from CUA in 1991, several new appointments to the Department of Theology have been of fine young scholars faithful to the magisterium, including Peter Casarella, Joseph Capizi, and John Berkman. Its new president, Daniel O'Connell, C.M., is also dedicated to making the University truly Catholic.

In 1993 Pope John Paul II issued his great encyclical on the moral life, *Veritatis splendor (The Splendor of Truth)*. This encyclical rooted Christian moral life in the following of Christ, but it was chiefly concerned with showing that the "teleologisms" known as "consequentialism" and "proportionalism," which denied that there are acts intrinsically evil by reason of their moral "object," i.e., what one intends to do here and now, are utterly incompatible with Catholic faith and with reason. After the encyclical was published I was asked by Father Ramón Lucas Lucas of the Legionaries of Christ in Rome to contribute an essay to a volume of essays on the encyclical in which I was asked to identify the theologians whose views were those repudiated by the encyclical. I wrote the article, which showed clearly that such theologians as Richard McCormick, S.J., Joseph Fuchs, S.J., and Louis Janssens indeed held the views rejected by John Paul II as incompatible with Catholic Faith. Father Lucas Lucas wrote to tell me that my essay did exactly what he had hoped and that he was sending a copy of it to all the priests of the Legionaries of Christ. Several months later, however, he wrote to tell me that my essay would not be included in the volume he was editing because that volume now included an essay by His Eminence Pio Cardinal Laghi, at that time President of the Pontifical Congregation for Catholic Education. Apparently Laghi's office would be embarrassed if my essay appeared in the volume inasmuch as some of the theologians whose views I identified as those rejected by *Veritatis Splendor* were theologians approved by Laghi's Congregation. I was naturally upset over learning this, but then Msgr. Caffarra agreed to publish my essay in the scholarly journal of the John Paul II Institute in Rome, *Anthropotes*. It was published under the title "Theologians and Theologies in the Encyclical *Veritatis Splendor*," *Anthropotes: Rivista di Studi su Persona e la Famiglia* 10.1 (1994).

In 1995 *Time* magazine featured Pope John Paul II on its cover as "Man of the Year." The accompanying story stressed that he loved to engage in philosophical and theological discussion. I thought that the Holy Father's argument to show that contraception is intrinsically immoral for married persons, although helpful in many ways, was perhaps not the best argument to use to show why contraception is always gravely wrong. He noted, quite rightly, that the marital act is meant to express their "gift" of themselves to one another, and that through contraception its "language" of self-giving was replaced by a contradictory language, namely, that of refusing to give of oneself. Although I could see merit in this reasoning, I did not think it the best one to use, and it hardly explains why it is morally wrong for *unmarried* persons to contracept. Moreover, in 1988, to commemorate the 20th anniversary of *Humanae vitae,* I had been privileged to be associated with Germain Grisez, Joseph Boyle, and John Finnis in writing a long article, " 'Every Marital Act Ought To Be Open to New Life': Toward a Clearer Understanding," which was published in both the *Thomist* and *Anthropotes.* In this essay we developed a line of reasoning Grisez had taken in some previous writings and rooted in the Christian tradition against contraception. This argument compares contraception to homicide; it recognizes the real difference between them, of course, but it stresses that the two kinds of acts are similar insofar as both are contra-life or anti-life kinds of action. This argument had been common among the Fathers of the Church (see, for instance, St. John Chrysostom's Homily 24 on the Epistle to the Romans) and was used by St. Thomas Aquinas (see his *Summa contra gentiles,* Bk. 3, ch. 122). It was central to the famous *Si Aliquis* canon used in canon law from the 12th century until 1917 and to the teaching of the *Roman Catechism,* popularly known as the *Catechism of the Council of Trent* (see Part II, chapter 7, no. 13), and it was also used by the leaders of the Protestant reformation (see John Calvin in his *Commentaries on the First Book of Moses Called Genesis,* chapter 38: 9, 10).

John Paul II himself, in some of his homilies, had noted that contraception is an anti-life kind of act. I wanted to urge him to focus on the anti-life nature of contraception in future writings, and I thus wrote him a letter, enclosing with it a picture of my extended family taken during the Christmas holidays of 1993 (it included my wife and me, our seven children, Michael's wife Monica and their children Christopher and Elizabeth, Mary Pat and her husband Andrew and their daughter Alexandra). I sent the letter and picture to the Pope's secretary, Msgr. Stanislaw Dziwisz, asking him to show the material to the Holy Father if he thought it proper; otherwise he should throw it into the wastebasket. Msgr. Dziwisz gave my letter with the enclosed picture to Pope John Paul II, who subsequently wrote a personal letter to me. Here I reprint the letter I sent along with the Holy Father's reply.

January 9, 1995

His Holiness
Pope John Paul II
Bishop of Rome
Palazzo Apostolico
00120 Vatican City State
Europe

Dear Holy Father:

I am sending this letter personally to you because you are not only a good and courageous pope but a great philosopher and theologian whose writings on marriage and the family and, in particular, on the beauty and truth of the marital act and the way contraception debases this act have been a marvelous help to so many men and women throughout the world.

The precise question I wish to take up is the evil of contraception and the arguments used to help people understand its grave immorality.

In your many writings on the subject you center attention on the truth that contraception falsifies the marital act, and you do so beautifully and forcefully. The marital act, whereby husband and wife, who have already given themselves unconditionally and irrevocably to one another in marriage, is a beautiful expression of their reciprocal gift of themselves as bodily, sexual persons, as male and female. It is through this beautiful union that God wills to give new human life, the life that, as St. Augustine said so long ago, is "to be lovingly received, nourished humanely, and educated religiously," that is, in the love and service of God and neighbor. As you rightly say, for example, in *Familiaris consortio,* 32, when married couples have recourse to contraception they act as "arbiters" of the divine plan and they "manipulate" and degrade human sexuality—and with it themselves and their married partner—by altering its value of "total" self-giving. Thus the innate language that expresses the total reciprocal self-giving of husband and wife is overlaid, through contraception, by an objectively contradictory language, namely, that of not giving oneself totally to the other. This leads not only to a positive refusal to be open to new life but also to a falsification of the inner truth of conjugal love, which is called upon to give itself in personal totality.

This is very true. Because of contraception the intimate bodily union between husband and wife is not a true marital act. In fact, I believe that a contracepted sexual act between husband and wife does not consummate marriage, because the marital act is an act that is meant to participate in the marriage, to actualize it, and to be open to the goods or blessings of marriage, whereas by contraception they have made their sexual union to be an act closed to these goods and blessings.

Nonetheless, and this is the matter that I wish to bring up, this argument, true as it is, does not precisely, I believe, show why contraception is an intrinsically evil act and why it is gravely immoral for fornicators and adulterers, as well as married couples, to contracept.

Although it is true that a married couple who contracept falsify their marital act and refuse to "give" themselves to one another unreservedly, I do not believe that married couples who contracept "intend," i.e., either choose as their means or intend as their "end," the "not-giving" of themselves. In fact, many fallaciously claim that they contracept precisely in order to give themselves to one another in the marital act. In other words, the "not-giving of self" that contraception causes is *praeter intentionem*. The "not-giving of self" is an effect or consequence of their contraceptive act and, at least ordinarily, is not within the scope of their intention.

As you rightly emphasize in *Veritatis splendor* (n. 78), and as St. Thomas rightly teaches, human acts are put into their species by their moral object, i.e., the precise object freely chosen, the end of the *voluntas eligens*. Thus contraception, I believe, is properly defined—as it is in *Humanae vitae*, no. 14—as "actus, qui cum coniugium commercium [et commercium nonconiugum] vel praevidetur, vel efficitur, vel ad suos naturales exitus ducit, id tampuam finem obtinendum aut viam adhibendam intendat, ut procreatio impediatur."

In other words, a person who contracepts intends, either as means or as end, to impede procreation. This precisely defines *what* the person, whether married or not married, is doing, and anyone who contracepts cannot not intend to impede procreation. Contraception, as you have noted in other writings, is an *anti-life* kind of act. As such, moreover, contraception is itself *not* a sexual act but one related to a sexual act. For instance, suppose the case of a father who judges that it would not be good for his married daughter to become pregnant. His daughter and her husband, for legitimate reasons, are living in her father's home. Both his daughter and her husband vehemently reject contraception and, indeed, are anxious to have their marriage blessed with the gift of life. But the father, who does not think that they should have a baby at this time, prepares breakfast and puts a contraceptive pill into his daughter's cereal. He is the one who is contracepting, not his daughter, because he is the one who freely chooses to do something, prior to his daughter's and her husband's freely chosen marital act, precisely to impede procreation, i.e., to impede the beginning of new human life.

You have, as I noted already, at times stressed the anti-life nature of contraception, e.g., in your homily at the Mass for Youth in Nairobi, Kenya, August 17, 1985 (in *Insegnamenti di Giovanni Paolo II*, vol. 8, part2, p. 453). I believe it would be good if you could emphasize the anti-life character of contraception more frequently in future addresses and documents. The argument that contraception falsifies and debases the marital act is a powerful one and has helped many to see the evil of contraception *for loving husbands and wives*. But contraception is an intrinsically evil act, and if fornicators and adulterers contracept they add to the malice of their behavior.

Moreover, if the anti-life nature of contraception is more clearly and forcibly brought to light, this will help people understand more clearly the deep connection between contraception and abortion. Contraception is indeed the gateway to the horrible evil of abortion, because the same anti-life attitude is expressed in them.

I hope that these reflections may be of some value to you. You are the greatest champion of marriage, the family, and the sanctity and dignity of human life in the world today. May God bless you and comfort you in your work. You are constantly in my prayers and in the prayers of millions.

Sincerely in our Lord,

William E. May
Michael J. McGivney Professor of Moral Theology

John Paul II Institute for Studies on Marriage and Family

PS. I have enclosed a picture of my family, taken at Christmas 1993, along with identification of family members. I ask your prayers for all of them.

    Some months later I received the follow letter in reply from the Holy Father:

March 13, 1995

Professor William E. May
John Paul II Institute for Studies on Marriage and Family
487 Michigan Avenue N.E.
Washington, D.C. 20017
U.S.A.

Dear Professor May,

    Thank you for your letter of January 9, 1995, and the kind message it contains.

    You speak of what I have been trying to explain in an age when it is difficult to make peoples and governments understand the intrinsic evil of abortion, while to many contraception seems a happy escape.

    Your stress on the anti-life character of contraception coincides with my new Encyclical on the "Gospel of Life," which shall soon appear. I hope you will be happy with it.

    It is good to hear that the Church's teaching on contraception has been a "marvelous help to many men and women throughout the world." It is not often that this teaching gets much praise.

    It is heartening to see a picture of a beautiful and happy family in full bloom. The Father is modestly hidden and quite difficult to find among his "sons like plants in full growth and daughters like corner pillars, cut for the structure of a palace," as Psalm 144 puts it.

    My blessing goes out to you, Professor May, to Mrs. May, and all your 7 children, including the present and future in-laws, and all the grandchildren.

Joannes Paulus II

I was naturally thrilled to receive this letter from the Holy Father. His encyclical on the "Gospel of Life" (*Evangelium vitae*), issued on the Feast of the Annunciation, March 25, 1995, does take up the relationship between contraception and abortion in no. 12. There the Holy Father does say that they are "fruits of the same tree," and he also emphasizes that "the negative values inherent in the 'contraceptive mentality' are such that they in fact strengthen this temptation [the temptation to have an abortion] when an unwanted life is conceived." Nonetheless in this number John Paul II also emphasizes that contraception, as an act specifically distinct from abortion, "contradicts the full truth of the sexual act as the proper expression of conjugal love" and is therefore "opposed to the virtue of chastity in marriage," whereas abortion "destroys the life of a human being" and thus "directly violates the commandment 'You shall not kill.'"

While this Encyclical does indeed note that contraception and abortion as fruits of the same tree are opposed to the good of life, the argument against contraception remains the one emphasizing how it violates conjugal love and chastity. I had hoped that the Holy Father would have given more emphasis to the anti-life nature of contraception. Nonetheless, this Encyclical of his is surely one of his greatest, and by God's kind providence the Holy Father read my letter, personally thanked me for it, and gave his blessing to me and my family. What more could one ask.

In 1995, when I was in Rome in May teaching at the Pontificia Univerisità della Santa Croce, I attended the STD defense by Father Donald Haggerty of New York at the Accademia Alfonsiana of his study on Jacques Maritain's idea of connatural knowledge of natural law. Father Haggerty gave a brilliant defense. After it he gave me the *dispense* of a Maltese professor of moral theology, Mark Attard, O. Carm., who taught at the Regina Mundi college where religious sisters from all over the world studied, among them Mother Teresa's Sisters of Charity. These *dispense* or professor's notes clearly showed that Attard, even after the publication of *Veritatis splendor,* defended the proportionalist method of making moral judgments and taught that contraception and abortion, for instance, could be morally justifiable under certain conditions. Father Haggerty had been given the *dispense* by a Sister of Mother Teresa's Sisters of Charity because Father

Haggerty had worked with Mother Teresa's Sisters in India before he was ordained. Father Haggerty then advised Mother Teresa not to send her Sisters to Regina Mundi because of the views of Father Attard. But when Mother Teresa told Cardinal Laghi that she intended not to send her Sisters to Regina Mundi in the future, the Cardinal persuaded her to keep her Sisters at Regina Mundi and defended Father Attard.

A few days later Father Haggerty, Father John Hardon, S.J., and I attended a celebration at a Roman Church where Mother Teresa was sending some of her Sisters to their mission. Father Hardon, who knew Mother Teresa very well, and I saw her after the ceremony and pleaded with her to meet us in Washington early in 1996 when she would be visiting her Sisters working at the House of Peace for individuals suffering from AIDs in the nation's capital. She agreed to meet us, and at the meeting Father Hardon and I convinced Mother Teresa that she should not send her Sisters to Regina Mundi but to some other educational institute in Rome.

It is, however, sad to know that theologians who dissent from magisterial teaching continue to teach not only in many US Catholic universities but also in some universities in Rome itself.

CHAPTER FOUR

CONCLUDING REFLECTIONS

I have been at the John Paul II Institute for Studies on Marriage and the Family since August 1991, and intend to remain teaching there until I fully retire in 2008 at the age of 80. For over 10 years I taught at least 5 and frequently 6 courses a year at different graduate levels—the Master's, the Licentiate (STL), and the doctorate (STD). In 2001 my superiors at the Institute decided that I should teach a reduced schedule of classes; thus now I usually teach only one course a semester, although I am sometimes asked to teach more. I teach whatever I am asked to do (ordinarily, a course in bioethics one semester and one on the redemption of human sexuality in another), and I continue with direction of licentiate and doctoral dissertations. At the Institute we have been blessed with fine students at all levels, and I have had the good fortune of directing many doctoral studies, several of them truly outstanding, in particular those by William Marshner of Christendom College, Rev. Paul deLadurantaye, head of the religious education department of the diocese of Arlington, Emmanuel Afunugo, who now teaches moral theology at St. Vincent's College and Seminary, Latrobe, PA, and Mark Latkovic, a layman whom I had taught at CUA and urged to attend JPII for his licentiate, which he wrote under the direction of the great Dominican theologian Benedict Ashley. Mark's doctoral study was a splendid study of the moral thought of Ashley. Married and the father of four, Mark is now professor of moral theology at Sacred Heart Major Seminary in Detroit. Here I cannot name all the wonderful students that I have had, both at CUA and JPII, but God has richly blessed me with fine students, men and women, lay and cleric—at JPII the great majority of our students are lay men and lay women, and it would be hard to find a finer group of intelligent, hardworking young men and women devoted to the Church and the saving truths it teaches than our students.

In 2006 two of my students completed very important doctoral studies: Father Brian Bransfield of Philadelphia wrote to show why persons of the same sex cannot marry, and Robert Plich, O.P., of Poland, a masterful presentation and critique of the widely influential work of Tom Beauchamp and James Childress on principles of bioethics.

The JPII Institute also has an excellent faculty. When I began teaching Carl Anderson, vice President and Dean, taught courses on marriage and the law. Carl is now the Supreme Knight of the Knights of Columbus, whose generous financial support underwrites the major expenses of the Institute. In 1991 Rev. Msgr. Lorenzo Albacete, a priest of great wit and profundity of thought, taught many different courses, among them one on the thought of John Paul II. Romanus Cessario, O.P. and Joseph A. DiNoia O.P., of the Dominican House of Studies where our offices and classes were held, taught courses on moral virtue and fundamental theology respectively. Father Francis Martin, without a doubt one of the greatest biblical theologians of our day, was at that time on the Dominican House faculty and taught courses on marriage in Scripture. He later served as a full-time member of our faculty until 2001. Professor Kenneth Schmitz, a world-renowned philosopher, after retiring from the University of Toronto, also joined us a full-time faculty member and for many years, until 2003, came each semester to teach concentrated courses for six weeks. He now comes for one semester each year. David Schindler, our current dean, joined us in 1992, and several of our graduates—Mary Shivanandan, Joseph Atkinson, and David Crawford—have become faculty members, along with Margaret Harper McCarthy, a graduate of the Roman Institute, Father Antonio López, a Spanish priest from Madrid who did his graduate work at Boston College, and most recently Father José Granados, another native of Madrid who finished his doctorate at the Lateran University in Rome. For several years Adrian Walker, a lay philosopher and graduate of the Gregorian University in Rome, taught for us. He recently had to leave us for personal reasons and we miss him very much.

There are now 10 John Paul II Institutes around the world, and through God's good providence I have had the opportunity to teach in several of them. I taught two-week intensive courses at the Institute in Kerala India twice (1998; 2000); in Ballina, Ireland three times (1999; 2000; 2001); and in Melbourne, Australia once (2002). Teaching in these sessions of the John Paul II Institute gave me the chance to meet wonderful people, in particular, the students and faculties of these academic institutes. In India the director is the apostolic and dynamic Father Joseph Alencherry; in Ireland, the acting dean was the warm and wonderful Mary Killeen (unfortunately, the Institute in Ballina was closed in 2003 for financial reasons; however, there is the possibility that another Institute will be founded in the British Isles, most likely in London). The first director of the Institute in Melbourne was Father Anthony Fisher, O.P. Father Fisher had studied in Oxford under John Finnis and at the Roman John Paul II Institute. He is without doubt an absolutely outstanding scholar— his writings are among the most superb I have come across—and a holy priest. He was appointed auxiliary bishop of Sydney, Australia in 2003. His academic leadership will be sorely missed. I am most happy to report that Father, now Bishop, Fisher, has been succeeded by Mgsr. Peter Elliott, a good friend whom I first met in Rome when he was working in the Pontifical Council For the Family. I have also lectured several times at the Roman campus of the Institute, doing so in Italian, and I am particularly grateful for the wonderful friendship and kindness of Msgr. Livio Melina, a brilliant moral theologian, and Professor Stanislaw Grygiel, who studied philosophy under Karol Wojtyla. Melina and Grygiel have come for many years to the Washington Institute to give a week of wonderful lectures much appreciated by our students. Early in 2006 Pope Benedict appointed Melina as the new president of the John Paul II Institute in Rome. For the past few years one of Melina's finest students, Father José Noriega, has been coming to the Institute in Washington. He is a wonderful friend, superb scholar, and excellent teacher.

As noted, I became a member of the Prelature of Opus Dei in the early 1990s and now serve as an adjunct professor at the Università Pontificia della Santa Croce (formerly the Collegio Accademico Romano della Santa Croce) in Rome, and offer an intensive two-week course there every other year. The students and faculty of that great University are a joy to work with, in particular my American colleagues Fathers Steve Brock and Robert Gahl (philosophy) and John Wauck (communications), and such wonderful scholars as Father Bernardo Estrada from Colombia (Scripture) and Hernan Fitté from Argentina. In Rome also I have come to know Kevin Flannery, S.J., the Oxford educated American Jesuit who serves as Dean of the faculty of philosophy at the Università Pontificia Gregoriana and whom I regard as my finest friend in Rome. Another great young Jesuit teaching at the Biblical Institute in Rome is Paul Mankowski, S.J., a person of enormous literary talents. Also now in Rome is Father Joseph A. DiNoia, O.P., who used to teach at the Washington Dominican House of Studies and offered courses for JPII students; DiNoia serves as sub-Secretary of the Congregation for the Doctrine of the Faith. Through God's providence this superb theologian has become a good friend. In the summer of 2005 I had the opportunity to teach intensive courses in bioethics at the School of Bioethics at the Ateneo Pontificio della Regina Apostolorum, under the direction of the Legionaries of Christ and to have time with some of their fine faculty members—Fathers Gonzalo Miranda, Joseph Tham, and Jose Maria Anton—and to meet many fine students from around the world.

God has thus given me the opportunity to travel considerably, frequently with my wife since our children have all left home, and thus to meet wonderful people in Italy, Spain, Australia, New Zealand, India, Ireland, and elsewhere.

In 2003 I was appointed Visiting Professor at the Institute for the Psychological Sciences in Arlington, VA. This Institute, operated by the Legionaries of Christ, is a marvelous educational establishment whose purpose is to integrate sound Catholic thought into the curriculum preparing men and women to become professional psychologists and therapists. It has an excellent faculty, headed by Dean Gladys Sweeney, and a fine student body. One of my responsibilities is to provide seminars for the faculty and doctoral students, and through his providence God has now given me the opportunity to meet and work with outstanding professors of the psychological disciplines—Paul Vitz, William Nordling, Anthony Palmer, Frank Moncher, Philip Scrotani, Christian Brugger and others. In 2003 I also became adjunct professor at the Notre Dame Graduate School of Christendom College and here too I can work with dedicated Catholic scholars, Dean Kris Burns, Sister Timothy Prokes, and others whose example means much to me.

Remembering Pope John Paul II

On April 2, 2005 our great pope John Paul II died. I have, in the previous pages, frequently recalled some of my own memories of him. I want here to share some others.

I first met Pope John Paul II when, as Karol Cardinal Wojtyla, he gave a talk on the freedom of the acting person at The Catholic University of America about a year before he was elected Pope. He had come at the invitation of Jude Dougherty, Dean of the School of Philosophy at The Catholic University where at that time I was teaching moral theology. Cardinal Wojtyla's talk was profound, and afterwards there was an opportunity for my wife Patricia and me to meet him. He had the marvelous ability to look a person in the eyes making him feel that he was the only person in the room, and his handshake was firm and strong.

The next time I saw him was in October 1979 on his first visit to the United States as Pope John Paul II. I was privileged to see him three times on this occasion, once at a Mass at St. Matthew's Cathedral, then at a convocation for academics from all around the United States held at the gymnasium of The Catholic University, and finally at the Capitol Mall on Sunday, October 7, when he celebrated Mass and gave one of the most powerful addresses of his entire pontificate, "'Stand Up' for Human Life!" I took five of my children—Thomas, Timothy, Patrick, Susan, and Kathleen—to the Mass on the Capitol Mall. My wife Patricia could not, unfortunately, come because of the flu, and our oldest son, Michael, then a student at Catholic University, was working. Our oldest daughter, Mary Patricia, was studying at Harvard University, but she had been able to see and hear John Paul II in one of his appearances in Boston and was thrilled that she could do so. The Mall was packed and the Pope gave an unforgettable homily on the preciousness of human life. In it he declared: "Nothing surpasses the greatness or dignity of a human person. Human life is not just an idea or an abstraction; human life is the concrete reality of a being that lives, that acts, that grows and develops; human life is the concrete reality of a being that is capable of love, and of service to humanity.... Human life is precious because it is the gift of a God whose love is infinite; and when God gives life, it is for ever."

Sadly, however, some people walked out on his homily when he affirmed that marriage is an indissoluble union and that husbands and wives should be generous in welcoming new human life and must be "open to" it in their conjugal acts.

In this narrative I have already had the opportunity to say something of the times I was privileged to see and be with John Paul II while I was a member of the International Theological Commission. The last time I saw John Paul II was on February 23, 2003, during the meeting of the Pontifical Academy for Life. I am not a member of the Academy, but that year I had given a paper on experimentation on human subjects to the members, and Bishop Elio Sgreccia, its vice-president, invited me to attend the audience the Holy Father granted to the Academy. This time John Paul II was confined to a chair, but his voice was still strong and he gave us a marvelous talk and afterwards each of us was able to come forward, shake and kiss his hand, and receive from him his loving look and a gift of the rosary.

John Paul II was a most remarkable person. His writings are among the most profound I have ever read, and I learn something new each time I read them. He had a fantastic personal charisma; he was able to make everyone who met him feel at home; his love for people, especially the weak and the poor, was palpable. I remember one time when I was among several thousand in St. Peter's Square in the year 2000 on a very humid October day on the occasion of a world meeting of the Holy Father with families. Different families from throughout the world were presented to John Paul II, seated; he loved to take children in his arms and kiss them, and several times he reached down to lift from a wheel chair a small crippled child whom he would embrace and bless especially.

He was without doubt the greatest champion of the dignity and preciousness of human life in our time and perhaps is unparalleled in the defense of human life in the history of the world. We will miss him. *Requiescat in pace.*

POPE BENEDICT XVI

I have already noted how gracious and courteous our new Holy Father, as Cardinal Ratzinger, was to me and others while I served on the International Theological Commission from 1986-1997, and in particular of his wonderful kindness to my wife Patricia when she accompanied me to Rome in October 1988, on our 30th wedding anniversary, and he arranged to have her as the guest of honor at the magnificent *pranzo* he gave for the members of the Commission.

I have since 1997 had other occasions to see the then Cardinal Ratzinger. The last time was in May, 2002, when I was teaching a two-week course at Santa Croce. Patricia was with me and I had arranged for a meeting with the Cardinal, who graciously gave me a good half hour of his time. I said to him, "Cardinal, you impress me as a person who is at peace with himself." To this he replied, "I am," and indeed he is. He has great inner tranquility precisely because he is a man of prayer and humility. He then said to me that it was my time to talk and that he would listen. I told him that the Congregation ought to resolve some issues heatedly debated by theologians—e.g., providing food/hydration to persons in the so-called "persistent vegetative state" (John Paul II on March 20, 2004 resolved this issue, I believe, despite the fact that some theologians reject his teaching), "rescuing frozen embryos," the GIFT (gamete intrafallopian tube transfer) method of generating human life (with others I hold that this is immoral because it "substitutes" for the conjugal act whereas others argue that it "assists" the conjugal act and is therefore licit), and other questions. When I finished Cardinal Ratzinger told me that the Congregation for the Doctrine of the Faith planned to issue a document, sort of a sequel to its 1987 *Donum vitae*, on these issues. Later I was appointed to one of four committees, under the leadership of Bishop Elio Sgreccia, now President of the Pontifical Academy for Life). These committees met during 2003 and by the end of

2004 were able to send to the Congregation their reports. It is not known, however, when the Congregation, now under the presidency of Archbishop William Levada, will issue a statement.

Ratzinger, now Pope Benedict XVI, was on that occasion in May 2002, simply marvelous. He is considerate, listens carefully and respectfully to others, and is above all a person "at peace with himself." He will be a wonderful pope.

THE CONTROVERSY IN 2006 OVER USE OF CONDOMS BY MARRIED COUPLES TO PREVENT TRANSMISSION OF HIV/AIDS

On April 21, 2006 Carlo Mario Cardinal Martini, retired Cardinal Archbishop of Milan, gave an interview in the Italian newsweekly *L'Expresso*, in which he maintained that it would be morally permissible for spouses to use condoms in order to prevent the transmission the HIV virus and the deadly disease of AIDS if one or the other spouse should contract the virus. The opinion he expressed was not new, for it had been advocated by some theologians as early as 1988 and had been strongly defended by the highly respected moral philosopher/theologian, Martin Rhonheimer, a priest of the Prelature of Opus Dei, in a July 2004 essay in the London *Tablet*. But now that a cardinal of the Church, and in particular one who had been favored by some to succeed Pope John Paul II, has voiced this opinion, it has caused many people to believe that the Holy See would indeed authorize such use of condoms in the near future, despite official denials that this was about to happen. As a result, many people are very confused about the matter. The situation today over this issue is analogous to the situation from about 1965-1968 regarding the Church's teaching on the intrinsic evil of contraception.

I hope that in the near future the Holy See will issue a strong and highly authoritative statement, perhaps by the Congregation for the Doctrine of the Faith, declaring that use of condoms by married couples is intrinsically evil and cannot be rightly chosen as a means of avoiding a disease.

In 1988 I wrote an essay to show why it is always immoral for spouses to engage in condomistic intercourse, even if the purpose for doing so is not contraceptive (for instance if the couple is known to be infertile because the wife has reached menopause and there would be no reason to contracept). After Rhonheimer's essay appeared in the London *Tablet* in 2004 I wrote a reply which, unfortunately, the editors of that journal chose not to publish. Since Cardinal Martini issued his unfortunate statement, I have sent letters to many Cardinals (among them Francis Cardinal Arinze, Alfonso Cardinal Lopez Trujillo, Carlo Cardinal Caffarra) who, I know, strongly oppose Cardinal Martini's position—urging them to encourage Pope Benedict to take strong action. In early May 2006 I sent a letter on this issue to Msgr. Georg Ganswein, personal secretary to His Holiness, along with a letter to give to our Holy Father if he, Msgr. Ganswein, deems it appropriate to do so.

Here I offer a brief argument to show why it is intrinsically wrong for spouses to use condoms while engaging in intercourse and why an appeal to the "lesser evil" cannot be used to justify such use.

Why the use of condoms by a spouse within marriage to prevent the transmission of HIV is intrinsically immoral*

Today some argue that use of a condom to prevent transmission of HIV between spouses would be permissible. Two reasons are given to support this view: (1) The use of condoms would not be contraceptive but would be intended to prevent the transmission of a potentially lethal virus. (2) One should permit a lesser evil in order to prevent a greater evil (in this case the death of a spouse).

Both of these reasons are incompatible with the Church's teaching about marriage and moral responsibility.

The first reason claims that condom use would be acceptable insofar as its use is not contraceptive in intent. It is possible that it might not be contraceptive in intent, although in the case of fertile couples this would be unusual, since in addition to not wishing to transmit HIV to a spouse they would also not wish to conceive a child with HIV. So they would also wish to prevent conception by

---

*The argument given here was developed through emails with Luke Gormally and John Finnis who are its primary creators.

using a condom. But even in those cases in which there is no contraceptive intent there is nonetheless a very serious and basic reason why condom use should not be adopted, namely, *condomistic sex would render the sexual activity of the spouses non-marital and the* **only** *genital act that respects the goods of human sexuality is the marital or conjugal act.*

In order for their sexual union to be marital, the act freely chosen by spouses must be a generative or procreative type of act – the type of act that, if the couple is fertile, can lead to the conception of a child (cf. *Code of Canon Law*, 1061, par. 1). In order for marital intercourse to be generative the husband must ejaculate into his wife's reproductive tract. But this is precisely what the deliberate, intentional use of a condom by spouses prevents. If intercourse is not of the generative kind, it can neither be marital nor have the unitive meaning intrinsic to marital intercourse. It fails to make the couple 'one-flesh'. It no longer speaks what John Paul II called 'the language of the body.' That is what is meant by the solemn teaching of *Humanae Vitae* #12 when it speaks of the *inseparability* of the unitive and procreative meanings of the marital act. To allow condom use within marriage even if there is no contraceptive intent would amount to an abandonment of the Church's fundamental teaching on what is required for sexual activity truly to realize the 'one flesh' unity of the couple.

The second reason offered for permitting condom use within marriage is a grave misunderstanding of what traditional Catholic teaching had in mind when it spoke of 'permitting the lesser evil'. Traditional use of the phrase related to the *toleration* or 'non-impeding' of the sins of *other* persons, but *not* to what one may licitly choose to do himself or herself. But those advocating the use of condoms by married couples as a way of avoiding the transmission of a disease and preventing death by HIV urge the *spouses* to choose the evil of condomistic, i.e., nonmarital, intercourse. But as seen above, such intercourse is *not* marital, and it is only to the marital act that spouses have a right. The Church has always taught that it is incompatible with an authentic sense of moral responsibility deliberately to choose what is known to be morally wrong, however good and desirable one's further purpose might be.

Many couples will reasonably conclude that if they accept the teaching that condomistic intercourse is intrinsically unchaste the only alternative for them is abstinence, which will indeed be a demanding cross for many of them. The Church's response to their situation should be to help them to embrace that cross in their lives as the instrument of their salvation. It is precisely in embracing what makes its appearance as the cross in one's own life that one experiences the power of the Resurrection. It is no part of the Church's mission to enjoin or allow behavior which defiles the sacred bond of marriage.

But it needs to be pointed out that abstinence is not necessarily the only reasonable alternative to condom use. While it is not reasonable for someone infected to *demand* intercourse when their spouse is unwilling to be exposed to the attendant risks, an uninfected spouse may have good reason to willingly take those risks, especially if the risks are low. And this may be true, for example, in the case of an infected husband if intercourse is confined to the infertile period of the woman's cycle and she does not suffer from lesions in the vagina, since infected seminal fluid will very likely be prevented by cervical mucus from entering the woman's upper reproductive tract.

Nor can a couple, one of whom is infected, be condemned as necessarily unreasonable for having intercourse with a view to having a child. For a child is a great good, and we rightly do not condemn couples seeking to conceive a child though they run some risk of begetting a child with a fatal condition. The risks of a child getting HIV are not high, especially if the woman is not at the time infected.

So spouses in considering their own situation are not necessarily confined to the alternative of complete abstinence to condom use.

In explaining the Church's teaching to individuals, pastors may readily concede that a particular couple could greatly reduce the risk of HIV transmission through the use of condoms. The essential case against condom use in marriage is that it is gravely unchaste, not that it is risky.

On the other hand, when pastors teach publicly that condom use is morally acceptable they should recognize that their message will influence a varied population whose behavior in using condoms may in the long run be significantly hazardous. One should bear in mind that studies of populations show that condom use for contraceptive purposes has a significant failure rate–where 'failure' means conception, which can occur only once a month, whereas HIV can be transmitted any day of the year.

The Church's ministry to couples, one of whom has HIV, is a challenging ministry. The challenge is evaded and they are betrayed if pastors think they can serve the good of couples and the good of their marriages by approving condom use.

At the end of May 2006 I received a letter from the Sub-Secretary of State of the Vatican informing me that my letter had been given to His Holiness, Pope Benedict XVI, who wished to thank me for it and who promised to consider carefully its contents.

THE BATTLE OVER CONTRACEPTION AND ITS SIGNIFICANCE

Most people in the Western world today, including Catholics, approve of contraception and practice it as a way of controlling birth. Young persons growing up in our culture for the most part consider contraception an intelligent way of coping with difficult problems; it is the "natural," "responsible" way to act. They find the Catholic Church's opposition to contraception a relic of a bygone age, unrealistic, impracticable.

This mentality, although common, is rooted in a dualistic understanding of the human person that regards the "person" as the subject conscious of himself or herself and capable of relating to other conscious selves and the human body as an "instrument" of the person. On this understanding bodily life is valuable insofar as being bodily alive is a necessary condition for experiencing "personal" values, i.e., values whose existence demands conscious awareness, love and affection for example. On this view the "personal" values of human sexuality are those that are consciously experienced, such as the tenderness and intimacy provided by sexual union. Our biological fertility does not, however, demand conscious awareness for its existence. As such it is not personal but rather part of the sub-personal world over which the "person" has been given dominion, and as "persons" we have the right to suppress this fertility by using contraceptives should its continued flourishing inhibit our participation in the "personal" values of human sexuality.

This dualistic view underlying acceptance of contraception likewise underlies acceptance of abortion, euthanasia, embryonic stem cell research, etc. On this view not all living members of the human species are "persons," but only those who are capable of conscious awareness; the unborn, the severely mentally crippled, and those in the "vegetative" state thus do not count as persons, who alone are the subjects of rights that must be recognized by the state.

From this it can be seen that contraception is the "gateway" to abortion and other grave offenses against the goodness of human life. Contraception paved the way for abortion, which is frequently considered a backup to failed contraception. All this explains why the Catholic Church is so opposed to contraception.

When God made man, he did not make a subject aware of itself as a self and capable of relating to other selves to which he then added a body as an afterthought. Rather, when he created man, "male and female he created them" (Gen 1.27). i.e., he created them as *bodily, sexual beings*, whose fertility is a blessing, not a curse. Moreover, when the eternally begotten Son of God, his "Word," became man to show us God's love for us and to redeem us, he became living flesh: "the Word became flesh" (Jn 1.14), he became *incarnate.*

Thus the Church's teaching on contraception goes hand-in-hand with the great truth that human persons are *bodily* persons and that every living member of the human species, the unborn as well as the born, the severely mentally impaired as well as the mentally gifted, is a person, a being of moral worth, a living image of the one and triune God.

"*I* HAVE SHIELDED YOU IN THE SHADOW OF MY HAND" (Is: 49:16)

I hope that this narrative shows how marvelously God's divine providence has cared for me and my family. Six of our children (Michael, Mary Patricia, Timothy, Patrick, Susan, and Kathleen) are now married, and our unmarried son Thomas is a doting uncle and commentator on classical music and has recently (2004) had his first book published, entitled *Decoding Wagner: An Invitation to His World of*

Music Drama. So good has God been to Pat and me that he has not only given us wonderful sons and daughters, but daughters-in-law (Monica, Alison, Mary Beth) and sons-in-law (Andrew, Gene, and James), and now 14 beautiful grandchildren (Christopher, Elizabeth, Alexandra [Sasha], Anastasia [Anna], Katya, Megan, Peter, Margaret Mary, Katie, Christina, Joaquin, Alexander, Juliet, and more recently, (January 19, 2006) Sophia with, God willing, more to come in the future. Amazingly, we even *like* all of our in-laws, and whenever we get together we tell each other how happy we are that our sons married their daughters or our daughters their sons—and they say the same to us.

     In his providence God cares for all of us. He sends each of us our own personal cross or crosses, but we must remember, as St. Josemaría Escriva has reminded us, that he is our Simon of Cyrene who will help us to bear whatever cross that each of us must take if we are to follow him. He has sent my older sister Rosemary many difficult crosses: the tragic death of their oldest son, the suicide of one of their sons-in-law and the devastating effect this had on one of their daughters and grandchildren, unfortunate marriages of other children, and recently the death of her husband Frank. Yet Rosemary, who was always my very kind and helpful big sister, is a woman of strong faith and deep humility, who loves God dearly. My younger sister Virginia (Jincey) finally left the Sisters of St. Joseph of Carondelet, but in his providence God sent her a wonderful widowed man, Robert Palmer, whom she married late in her life and with whom she is most happy.

     Indeed, God in his providence has richly blessed me and my family. He is truly our best and wisest friend, who gives all of us the vocation to holiness, to sanctity, and to each of us a unique personal vocation which we are to discern with his never-failing help and carry out in order to participate, as he wants us to, in his redemptive work.

PRÉCIS OF OFFICIAL CATHOLIC TEACHING

In the mid 1980's George "Pat" Morse, founder of Catholics Committed to Support the Pope, was introduced to Mario Cardinal Ciappi, O.P., John Paul II's personal theologian. Rome. He told the Cardinal of his plan to publish a series of books that would present accurately and in readable form substantive summaries of the authoritative teaching of the Church on a wide range of issues. The Cardinal immediately recognized the tremendous significance of Pat's proposal and encouraged him to go ahead with it. Eduoard Cardinal Gagnon, P.S.S., then president of the Pontifical Council for the Family was also excited about the idea and introduced him to Father Peter Elliott, an Australian theologian working with him.

On returning to Washington, Pat told then Archbishop James Hickey of his idea. Hickey too was enthusiastic and advised Pat to enlist my help. My job was to identify the areas of Catholic teaching on faith and morals that would be covered as well as the Magisterial documents concerned with them and also to supervise and ensure the accuracy and comprehensiveness of the work of graduate students of theology who would prepare the summaries of the documents. Father, now Msgr., Elliott, provided excellent "background" statements to every document included in the different volumes. Elliott has now returned to Australia where he serves as Director of the John Paul II Institute for Studies on Marriage and Family.

The 13th and final volume of this remarkable series will be published in the fall of 2006. 3500 pages of text provide excellent and accurate summaries of Catholic teaching.

I. *Faith, Revelation, and the Bible* (1990)
II. *Christ the Lord, True God and True Man* (1991)
III. *The Church* (1992)
IV. *Marriage, Family and Sexuality* (1992)
V. *The Sanctity of Human Life* (1993)
VI. *The Social Teaching of the Church* (1993)
VII. *The Ordained Priesthood* (1994)
VIII. *Worship and Sacraments* (1994)
IX. *The Christian Call to Personal Perfection* (1996)
X. *Catholic Education* (1996)
XI. *Marian Devotions and the Last Things* (1997)
XII. *Supplementary Magisterial Documents* (2000) [documents from 1997 to 2000]
XIII. *Supplementary Magisterial Documents II* (2006) [documents from 2000 to 2006]

The entire set of Volumes I through XII can be purchased for $135.00 from CCSP, 9402 Stateside Court, Silver Spring, MD 20903.

It has been a privilege to help Pat Morse, who will be 90 years old March 17 2007, and his wife Margaret, on this great project of service to the Church.

William E. May

-REQUIEM PRESS-

REQUIEM PRESS was launched in the spring of 2004 to publish books which illustrate God's action in the history of mankind and man's response to God.

Through both original titles and newly typeset and updated reprints of hard-to-find classics, REQUIEM PRESS hopes to enliven hearts and stimulate minds for a deeper love of God and His Church. Understanding the events of the past and their importance today can help us defend the Faith and chart a course according to God's will in the present.

At REQUIEM PRESS we have a special devotion of praying for the *Holy Souls in Purgatory*. This devotion of the Church Militant in participating in the Communion of Saints has been neglected in recent years in some quarters. By our special booklets dedicated to prayers for the *holy souls*, we hope to revive this devotion so that the Church Suffering's deepest longings for Heaven can be realized.

We do not solicit donations for our work, but ask for your prayers and to spread the word about our books.

For your free catalog and a free *holy souls* prayer booklet, please call:

Toll-free: 1-888-708-7675

or write:

REQUIEM PRESS
P.O. Box 7
Bethune, SC 29009
www.requiempress.com